CW00544092

THE ALCHEMY OF THE HEART

Reshad Feild's spiritual search has taken him around the world to Zen monasteries in Japan, the Himalayas and to Turkey where he studied the Sufi mystical traditions and was initiated into the order of the Mevlevi Dervishes.

He has been in turn a popular singer, an antique dealer and stockbroker. Throughout the 1970s he ran schools in human transformation in Britain, Canada and America. A professional geomancer, Reshad was granted his doctorate in psychological counselling in 1983. He is the author of several other books which have been described as classics of contemporary spiritual literature.

By the same author

The Invisible Way
The Last Barrier
Steps to Freedom
Here to Heal
The Travelling People's Feild Guide
Footprints in the Sand
Breathing Alive

For Lynne —
With love & Blessings
on your Journey.
from
Reshad.
16th July 2010.
Totnes.

The Alchemy
of
the Heart

RESHAD FEILD

Compiled and Edited by
MATTHEW SHOEMAKER

ELEMENT
Shaftesbury, Dorset ● Rockport, Massachusetts

© Reshad T. Feild and Matthew Shoemaker 1990

First published in Great Britain in 1990 by
Element Books Limited
Longmead, Shaftesbury, Dorset

First published in the USA in 1992 by
Element, Inc. 42 Broadway, Rockport, MA 01966

Reprinted 1992

Cover calligraphy by Ngakpa Chögyam
Cover Design by Brian Keeble
Designed by Roger Lightfoot
Typeset by Selectmove, London
Printed and bound in Great Britain by
Billings Ltd., Hylton Road, Worcester

British Library Cataloguing in Publication Data
Feild, Reshad
   The alchemy of the heart.
   1. Spirituality
   I. Title   II. Shoemaker, Matthew
   291.4

Library of Congress Catalog Card Number
available

ISBN 1–85230–171–6

Foreword

To write a foreword to a book that, in a sense, was not written but was transcribed and edited, is difficult. However, Matt Shoemaker, John Baldock and my wife, Penny Feild, have completed an extraordinary work to bring what was, after all, a distillation of thousands of hours of talks into, I hope, a readable experience! To me the word has always been able to contain, hold and transmit the Living Truth. Very sincerely I offer this book as an expression of my own personal experience and not as a second-hand copy of information I never understood.

If you held the hand of Truth, what would it be? Would it be that of your friend or a lover? Would it be separate from life or could it be the touch of a blade of grass moving in the wind by the river's bank? When we touch the hand of Truth it is God's hand, reaching out to us from before time.

Reshad Feild
Zurich, Switzerland
May, 1990

Dedication

This book is dedicated to all those seekers after Truth who are prepared to surrender that which stands between them and the Truth Itself.

Contents

Editor's Preface

This book is a collection of teachings from classes and workshops given by Reshad Feild over the last fifteen years. I gathered the material from a huge assortment of tape recordings, then edited and organized it all according to various themes. It was like working with pieces of a puzzle. In the beginning I had no idea how the book would come together, but after persevering through many stages of doubt and frustration, the pattern of the book finally began to come into shape.

The content of this book is universally relevant. It not only speaks from the heart of Sufism but reveals the essence of the spiritual path itself. It is a book that can plant significant ideas and reveal helpful pointers for those with an open mind and open heart. Any true path requires personal effort, study, and assimilation of the ideas into actual practice. Study/work groups are very useful for this purpose, and one can also benefit from contact with others having a similar intention. I would recommend that anyone who is interested in developing a greater understanding and application of these teachings should contact the school under Reshad's direction.

I am very grateful for having had the opportunity to make this book a reality, because I know it can lead readers toward an understanding of themselves and the purpose of their lives. This book will live on for generations to come as a testimony of truth. Special thanks need also be given to John Baldock and Penny Feild for their excellent work of final editing. And of course a special thanks to Reshad for making this all possible.

MATTHEW SHOEMAKER
June 24, 1990

1

The Quest

Your desire for God is God's desire for you.

What is a question? What is the quest? The quest of a seeker is the quest of all seekers. Yet none of us will have exactly the same quest because we are all unique individuals within the One Reality. The goal may be the same in the end, if we ever reach it, but our approaches will be different because we each begin from a unique place. Each search will travel a unique path simply because it is impossible for any two people to have the same experiences along the way and, of course, the search will be made on our own, even if we choose to be with a certain group for the journey into the unknown. The search is your own because nobody can do it for you. The speed of the journey depends upon your motive and the quality of your question. And it is very good to question your motive.

Usually we become seekers from a deep yearning to know what life is all about, and with that there inevitably comes a sense of frustration in the face of all the greed, hatred and stupidity around us. We find in the world and in ourselves so much of what holds us back from realising our journey's end. We want to change the world and we want to better ourselves that we may serve life better. It is hard to understand why so many people abuse each other and the planet we live on. We might even sense the urgency of the situation in which it is obvious that a major cycle of history is coming to a close. With this we see the fear and pain increasing as more and more of the past dissolves in front of us. We want things to be easy, but we cannot just go along with the tide of a dying world without doing something about it all. But it is difficult to find a spiritual path that satisfies the deepest yearning of our hearts.

Do you really want to know the truth, or do you just want to find something to satisfy your self-righteousness? Deep within the heart of all people is the longing to know the Truth, but so often this gets covered over by the many attractions and distractions in life. If you want something you have to ask. Do you want realisation? No one can give you that, but you need to ask and you need to want it very, very much.

The real questions we have are not just about us. This is our illusion of separation. The deeper questions are those shared by all seekers from the beginning of time. Even at this moment everyone in the world is here with you; there is nothing outside your armspan. In this realisation, the responsibility of this Work is tremendous. It is said that whenever you pronounce the name of God correctly another human being is turning to God, and whenever you make love consciously a child is being born consciously. So the quest is not just about you. What is your true motive in this search? Suddenly we are in perplexity when we question this because we haven't looked clearly at our motives, nor at who is really searching. The motive may at first come from an egocentric space, but essentially it comes from love because love is the cause of all creation. Our search may actually be God's search for us.

Without exception we approach this path from 'centric space'. Centric space is when 'I' am looking for enlightenment, 'I' am looking for the truth, 'I' have this pain, this block, and 'I' am looking for the way out of it. This is one of the potential traps because when one looks for 'self-enlightenment' or 'self-development' one is merely expanding one's concept of the 'self'. If you don't yet know who you are, you cannot find out by developing or expanding an old concept of yourself. This is merely expanding the centric space of 'I' or 'me'. Of course one can have lovely experiences from this space, experiences of light and higher states, but it is impossible to find the true self unless one breaks through this centric space.

We have to break out of the concept of 'I', the centric space of 'I', and open up in a new way to what is coming into our being. The way to do this is through 'reversing space', by realising that we are continuously becoming from pure being, out of which can come self-knowledge. It is as though we were being spun into being out of this very moment. When we give up the concept of 'I am searching' or 'I know', then there is only continuous becoming. What we are is the composite manifestation of a moment of time. We are becoming from being. The Sufis say, 'There is no creation in the relative world; there is only the becoming of being.' Here, we cease to have the centric sense that we are the cause of anything. We know our dependence upon God. In this 'peripheral space' we see that we do not really do anything. Instead, life is the becoming of being.

Out of these two spaces—centric space and peripheral space—and the alchemical process between them, something can come out of this moment that was not there before. This is the key to knowledge. In the Koran knowledge is symbolised by milk because it is a food that is derived from an alchemical process. Without transmutation there would be no milk, no knowledge. So it is through both centric space and peripheral space that creation comes into being. When the two spaces merge consciously in man, then love and desire, God and man, the little 'I' and the greater 'I AM', come together in an alchemical marriage.

The key for breaking out of centric space lies within a question. We need to ask a real question from our centric space. We cannot come upon this Way, which is invisible and has no label, unless we ask. We will not find it if we do not ask. We will not find it unless we want it more than anything else. Whether we ask verbally or deep inside our being, we need to ask. If the question is continuously asked, a deep passion burns in the heart, and from this burning the answer is given. The more intensely we ask from the heart, the greater the burning destroys that which asks. That which asks, from centric space, is melted by the very question itself. If the time is right the answer is given instantaneously. If the time is not right it will be given later, but without a real question nothing can really be given.

At this moment there is a question. In every moment there is a question if we can listen. With every heart beat of our lives there is a question. Such a question could be 'Who am I?' That is an eternal question. The answer lies within the question itself, and the one who asks it can only unfold the answer by living in the question. To live in the question is to live at the very point of life. It is to live with intensity, an intensity of wakefulness and passion. If you get bored or tired of life, it is because you have lost the question. If you are bored or in resentment or envy, then at least admit to the situation you are in and find the question in this. You are the embodiment of the question and that is a wonderful challenge. It is much better that I challenge you with a question than leave you with an answer, because there is no ultimate answer.

The first way to help somebody is to get them into the question, to get them to look at their own deepest question. Ultimately, you are the question and you become the question for other people because you become a mirror for them. Look at Jesus, for example. He was a marvellous question, wasn't he? A real teacher is a question, or becomes a question for you. He becomes the mirror of your own question, of your own life.

There are two things that we need more than anything else at this time in history. One is the ability to listen and the other is the ability to ask a question. Sometimes I sit in front of hundreds of people and when we have a 'question and answer' period nobody asks a real question. Most people merely want to talk, or they want to attract attention, or express how important they are or how unimportant you are. An actual question from the heart, not an intellectual question, is not possible for them, mainly because they do not want to listen. Listening requires effort and a desire to know, and so does asking a question.

We need to learn what it means to ask a question, not from the head but from the heart. If we were to live every moment in a question, we would know that the answer is in the question itself. Consider what it would mean if the educational system was based upon asking questions, instead of merely giving answers. I don't mean just intellectual questions, though these are necessary in their own way, but real questions of the heart. How often do people ask real questions from the heart? The educational system actually prevents individuals from asking a real question from the heart. It is based upon intellectual questions and intellectual answers. And people become very adept at this, until finally they receive a piece of paper saying that all the right questions have been answered. It is frightening that we can study and even teach throughout our lives without ever having asked a real question from the heart. Maybe near our death we will finally ask a real question, rather than thinking we already know the answer.

Seldom do we ask a real question, but it is only in the asking that real change can come about in our lives. A question implies that we do not know the answer but want to know the answer. This state of humility is necessary. It is also true to say that if we did not already know the answer deep inside we would not be asking the question in the first place. So the question also implies an intuition that there is an answer, that an answer lies within the question. We need to open up to the question and allow the answer to unfold itself in its own time, instead of asking a question and jumping to the first conclusion that comes to mind. In this way the question becomes an opening for insight and change in our lives. It is possible to live within the question itself but this takes courage, because it is much easier to presume that we know the answer rather than allowing the answer to unfold itself.

Only through the question can we allow the opening for real change to occur. A part of us may not want to hear the answer, or will only hear what it wants to hear. It wants to remain with its conditioning and preconceptions, doing the same things over and over again in slightly different ways. Change is a step into the unknown and a real question leads us into the unknown. It takes a tremendous amount of courage and trust to live completely in the question.

A real question comes from our pain which, on the highest level, is the pain of separation from God. And we can only receive the answer to our inner question, or prayer, when we are open and awake to the answer manifesting itself in this very moment. We need to pay attention, which means we need to give our full attention to the answer manifesting in whatever way it is given. We also need tremendous perseverance. We cannot live life passively; we need to search and struggle with a great degree of intensity and passion. The intention in our question needs to be strong and alive, or else that part of us that does not want to change or wake up will distract us from reaching our destination. We need to remember the question in order to find the truth that beckons us and not presume to be given the answer without pursuing the question. Little by little, that which does not want to know can be assimilated into that which does know. Finally, the pain of separation, which led us into the question in the first place, can be transformed into the realisation of Unity.

Jesus said, 'Seek and ye shall find.' We need to seek passionately and with humility, the humility of one who prays with all their heart for a portion of understanding in order to be of service. We accept that there is only One God, in whom we pray and by whom we are guided along the straight path to self-knowledge and service. We know that God is the only knower, and we ask passionately with honest humility to be granted a portion of this knowing.

In the realisation of our ignorance and our dependence upon God, we passionately desire to go home to Him, to be One with Him. Through prayer, and through a gradual dissolving of the illusion while essence remains, we come to realise that God has no other mouth but ours, no other eyes but ours, no other ears but ours and no other hands but ours. Then we go a stage further and realise that there is nothing but God: everywhere we turn there is the face of

God. We then go even further to realise that it is God who knows Himself in us. These are all steps in our awakening, but we need 'desire' to keep going. So it is said, 'Take one step towards God and He takes ten towards you.'

At first we may desire knowledge for ourselves or desire 'spiritual development', but then we realise that we cannot do it for ourselves because this self, as separate from the whole, is an illusion which actually dissolves with true self-knowledge. The greatest danger on the spiritual path is to believe that there is something to achieve. This is to be stuck in the relative world. It is only the relative 'I' that can achieve something for itself. But in essence you can achieve nothing for yourself that is not already inherent in the heart, waiting to be realised. It is desire that leads us on the path of return, which is really God's desire in and for us. Within our prayer, or within the sounding of His name, we are turning towards Him, opening up to Him (Him, meaning beyond he or she), and at the same time there can be the realisation that He is turning towards us. The yearning with passionate desire for God is actually God's yearning for us. Your desire for God is God's desire for you, all of you.

It is said in the Koran, 'We have not known Thee as Thou shouldst be known.' Ultimately, there is no end to the search, because that would be a limitation on God, the subject of the search. We desire to know God and desire to know the truth, yet if we were to see Him as He should be known, it would be the end of the whole search. If we all knew God perfectly it would be the end of this world, because the purpose of life in this world would already be completed. Life takes time to unfold in this world though sometimes we want it to happen more quickly. The tree does not want to take years to grow. It wants to shoot up to the sun in one moment. Fortunately for us it does take time, and so we have beautiful trees that give us oxygen, wood and shade.

We do not know God as God knows Himself, but God knows Himself through us. Remember the saying, 'I was a hidden treasure and I loved to be known, so I created the world that I might be known.' The world was made for man to know himself, which is God knowing Himself through us. Some will know and some will not. Mevlana Jalaluddin Rumi, the great thirteenth century Persian poet and mystic, said that the world is held in balance by those who know and those who do not. This does not mean that the numbers are equal. Only a few may know, but they hold a greater weight in the world. The more one knows the more responsibility one has because one must then 'carry' more people and 'carry' more of the weight of the world.

Yet however much one knows, the thirst does not die. In humility we must continually thirst for and continually drink of the Spirit. In each moment we die and in each moment we are reborn. In each moment we must completely surrender and yet be awake to the presence of God. We cannot be complacent for even one second. This doesn't mean that life has to be too serious but we can realise that there is always more to unfold, and it cannot unfold unless we are ready and willing to receive what needs to be known in each and every moment.

2

Knowledge

Our capacity for knowledge depends upon our degree of emptiness.

I have been involved with what is sometimes called the Way for over thirty years and still people ask me what it is about. It cannot be explained or understood by the mind because the mind lives in comparison. The Way cannot be limited by any belief system; it can only be known in the heart of the seeker.

If we enter this Way we do not need a label, because the Way does not have any specific form. It adapts itself to the needs of the moment. The form of the Way may change according to the time and place where it manifests on the planet, but don't be fooled by the form. See the meaning within it. We have to learn to look beyond the appearance of things.

Many people do what I call 'teapotting'. They stare at the 'teapot' and forget to drink the 'tea'. The teacher is like the spout of the teapot, and the function of the spout is to pour the tea into empty cups. Don't just come to look at the teapot or the spout. The purpose of the teapot is to hold and pour the tea, and the purpose of the cup is to receive and drink the tea.

Try to not get caught up in the form in any situation; learn to see what is being taught through the form in each moment. Everything that happens has some inner meaning, if you could only see it. If you can trust you will be given exactly what you need, because in this trust you are sufficiently open and empty to receive what you need. If you can come to this Way or, let us say, if you can come to life with open hands, you will get exactly what you need. But if you think you already have it, or if you come with one hand open and the other holding the past behind your back, then you will receive very little and probably go away in disappointment.

To come into the Way we have to love very much and we have to be willing to sacrifice a lot. We have to be willing to sacrifice our opinions in order to find the truth. The truth cannot live in the same room with anything else. We have to empty ourselves completely. We have to be willing to step into the unknown and trust that the truth will be revealed. The travellers of the Way have come to realise their total dependence upon God, which is real freedom. Anything else is an illusion of freedom. All the concepts of oneself, of God, of the Way, and all the theories of spiritual development and self-importance lead ultimately to disillusionment. The only freedom is through the realisation of our dependence upon God and our willingness to surrender all that we think we are.

We need to realise that we are really nothing, that we are non-existent except in God. Our problems lie in our belief that we are self-important, when, in fact, we are merely vehicles for the manifestation of the Spirit with the possibility of fulfilling a function within this Work. That is all we are. This brings about a true humility, and through humility we can be fully open to the Spirit, or the will of God. 'Humility' is a state of awareness ready for action. But usually we do nothing because we are so absorbed in the illusion of our own self-importance (and this can include our identification with apathy, self-pity and fear) that we cannot hear or see the will of God. We also need to beware of false humility, which means trying to be humble so we can gain something for ourselves. It is the difference between praying so that we can get to God and praying in the realisation that there is only God. In humility we realise that we are not something separate from God, but are one with God and dependent upon God for all knowledge.

Divine guidance brings us to a point of perplexity. This is the point where we just do not know. It is possible to be at this point and be completely sane. It comes about through humility and brings about the possibility of freedom. Perplexity is not the same as confusion. Perplexity comes from an opening of the heart in the realisation that we simply do not know. God is the great secret. If we are completely honest with ourselves we can realise that we do not really know anything, let alone what God is or who we are. It is possible to come to this point, but we have to be completely honest to get there. It takes a lot of courage. Courage is a quality that every man and woman needs in order to step into the perplexity of knowing that we do not know, which can then lead to the truth.

I have found that the most difficult people to help are those who come with definite beliefs about themselves and the nature of life. One of their favourite concepts is the belief in 'reincarnation'. Transformation is very difficult if you're stuck in the concept of reincarnation. It just doesn't exist, and if you hold on to that belief you cannot come into union with God because it takes you away from the knowledge of unity. Many people get upset with me when I say this because they are so attached to this concept of reincarnation. 'Chanelling' is another one of the concepts that takes us away from the truth of unity. Chanelling can divide us. It can create separation because there is 'you' and all of the many entities in the invisible worlds. First you are chanelling this one, then that one, and meanwhile you don't even know who 'you' are. Again, it can take us away from unity.

I'm not here to make you feel better about your pet beliefs. I am here to get you here. But how can you be here when you are thinking about some other lifetime? All these theories concerning reincarnation and past lives often take people away from facing themselves in the present moment, and yet it is only here that real healing can come about. Real transformation can only be in the present moment, and you can't be in the present moment when you are thinking about the past. 'What' do you think is reincarnating? You? Who is that? First find out who 'you' are. People say 'I' so presumptuously: 'I am this' or 'I was that'. Once you know yourself, the idea of reincarnation will not need to exist. As all great teachers have said, 'First, know thyself.'

Do you know who you are? In this tradition we say that you do not become a traveller on the Way until you know who you are. We do not even enter the Way until we know who we are, and that is a big leap which most of us have yet to take. First we must have the aspiration to begin looking for the road of truth. Then, if we find it we need tremendous courage to enter upon the Way. It is not an easy path. It takes a lot of hard work, a lot of love and a lot of patience, but eventually we are led to freedom. It is so easy to become complacent or to think we have arrived at the final truth. One of the greatest pitfalls is thinking we are on the Way when in fact we have not yet even begun.

In each moment we are given the circumstances which can lead us into realisation. Each moment is different in the relative world. No two moments can ever be the same. In each moment we are given something that no one else in the world has ever been given, and if we are awake and can learn from this moment then we move further towards realisation of the truth. Yet we cannot receive what we need if we are in comparison or judgement. The truth of life can be known by any human being in the world, but we rarely face that truth without comparing it to something that we think should be real. The food of the mind is thought and comparison. This can create a real hell in the mind because every negative thought or value judgement holds us in that prison of our own creation. And it affects everyone else in the world. You become free when you live in freedom, and then you free others. If you can live for the freedom of others you become free yourselves. But you have to pay for this with your own blood, with your own sacrifice, and then you become a willing slave of God, which is real freedom.

When we commit ourselves totally to life, we are given everything we need to become complete in unity of God. We might ask ourselves if we are committed to life. Every time we ask ourselves this question we will wake up. It is very useful to keep asking the question. We are useful to

God only if we are here, but only partially useful if we are only partially here.

We need to be fully here and in the present moment, wherein lies the key to transformation. Everything is here in potential in this one present moment, which unfolds continuously in different ways. We need to come into this understanding, not with the intellect, but in the depth of our being. Obviously we need commitment to bring forth the potential within us. The moment is like a window opening, then closing. Each moment an opportunity knocks, then is gone. Inevitably we waste a lot of time, and it is said that wastage is the only sin. But the past is already gone; there is no time for regrets. The only time is now. This is the time to be awake to the moment and the opportunities in front of us.

There is no time to waste. Do not wait around for something to happen. Do not wait for the saviour to appear, or for enlightenment, or for reincarnation. Do not wait for death. We do not have time to wait because the only time is now and the only time to realise the truth is in this moment. There is no other moment. The Path is always alive and it is always here in this moment, so one needs to be very humble in order to see what the moment teaches. The Path is right here in front of us and we are here to serve it. We may not know what our destiny is on this planet but we can allow it to work through us.

Never presume that you know anything completely. Be awake to what you are given in each moment, without judgement, without comparison, and be awake to what you can give. Do not get caught in the form. Do not get caught in agreeing with each other's illusions or opinions or complaints.

We can remind and help each other to wake up to a continuous state of surrender in the present moment. In surrender we can act from knowledge. We have to surrender in order to be awake and receive knowledge. Remember that knowledge is given and not acquired.

Of course study is still important, because study opens us up to receiving knowledge. It prepares us for the moment of knowing, when real knowledge can be given.

Nobody can do this for us, but we can be instruments for one another. We can help each other to be receptive to knowledge. Knowledge comes from a world beyond that which we normally listen to or see. Each of us can help bring forth this knowledge and be instruments for its awakening.

This requires study, which I define as the 'distillation of truth' from that which we are studying, whether it be sacred books or life itself. We must begin from the point of humility in the realisation that we are ignorant, and must never presume that we know anything unless that knowledge is given to us directly. There is inevitable struggle in this because there is that which does not want to learn or understand. Knowledge can bring about real change in one's life and there are parts of us which fear that change. We will need to struggle with ourselves to stay awake and be open to learning. We can receive knowledge and we can receive help along the way if we can remain open in trust and allow something from a higher world to enter our being. It takes trust. It takes humility.

Humility is that acceptance of not knowing, whereas the ordinary mind presumes that it knows and usually presumes that it knows more than most other people. We can practise being humble by first realising that we do not know. Even a teacher should be the eternal apprentice to truth and always be awake to knowledge. A teacher is someone who has discovered how to be a good pupil. It is true that the soul is a 'knowing substance'; there is a 'knowingness' within us but it needs to be awakened and not presumed, and this requires struggle and humility. In humility we need to study and keep on studying. This does not mean that we need more information or facts, or that we need to be 'intellectual' about study. What we do need, which is the reverse of the western system of education, is to be open to the guidance from sacred teachings and living teachers so that we are awake to the knowingness within.

Seek ye knowledge, and remember that knowledge can come to us in many ways, through roses or through human beings. Before knowledge there needs to be respect (from _respectare_, which means to see again). Respect gives us the capacity to know, and capacity ultimately has to do with emptiness of opinions and preconceptions. We most often think of fullness as the goal in life. There are many ways available which offer some kind of fulfilment and they fill people up with all kinds of practices and concepts. We have a cup and we think that it should be full of something to fulfil its purpose. But the 'cup' of the heart of the Sufi is dependent upon the capacity of its own emptiness. This way is the path of emptiness. It is not a path of systematised dogma. Only when we are empty can real knowledge be given.

Our capacity for knowledge depends upon our degree of emptiness. If we are full of our opinions and concepts about what is real then we will interpret whatever we hear and experience rather than distilling the essence of truth in what we are given. True understanding requires us to be fully in the present moment and the capacity for this depends upon our degree of emptiness.

To be empty is to reach a point where we do not think at all, for thinking is what gets in the way. Thinking controls us and wavers our attention from the present moment. But we can learn how to use the energy contained within thought consciously, which is different from being swayed hither and thither by our scattered thoughts.

It takes real work to be completely empty, empty of thoughts and opinions, judgements and false motivations. It takes time and effort. We don't have time to waste. So often we talk and talk, gossiping about other people and about things we do not yet understand. This is a hindrance to ourselves and others. We end up falling into patterns as a result of repeating our opinions. And the patterns are most often unconsciously those of our past, and come from our parents and ancestors. There is no freedom in this.

When we come into this Work we come under new laws. We have to be more careful about what we say and do, because it has a greater effect upon the whole. The further we go on in this Work the more careful we need to be; the results of what we think and do carry further in time and space. What does gossip do? It carries an opinion across the world. You find something out about so and so, and you tell someone else your opinion of this, and he tells yet another person about his opinion of your opinion of what might or might not have been, and so on. This is no exaggeration. It is usually much worse, and much more confusing. What are we creating? More thought, more opinions, more veils covering the truth. Pir Vilayat Khan once said, 'When you judge another you humiliate that person and veil yourself.' How many times have we been veiled, when life seems grey and worthless? We probably blamed outside forces for this, but was it because we became veiled ourselves through our judgements, opinions or gossip?

We cannot completely know what it is like to be another person. Everybody is unique, and we should respect that uniqueness. So often we play games with other people about what we think or feel they should be or do. We play games with each other about what we think is right and about what we think is the truth. We hear a little bit of what might be true then we add a lot of our imagination to it. Then we talk about it until we begin to forget that we really don't know what we are talking about. We really know very little but believe we know a lot. It is easy to deceive oneself, and this is why we need to be scrupulously honest with ourselves. When we realise how very little we know, then maybe we can begin to ask the right questions which will finally help us to know more of the truth.

3

The Path

The journey is long and there are many struggles along the way, but we have to persevere and keep on going.

We enter this Path out of need, and the need is to know ourselves and what this life is all about. We come across certain ideas or we experience certain things which lead us to question where we are going and what we are meant to do. This is the beginning of the Path and, if we are willing to persevere in the question, we will find ourselves upon the greatest journey there is. We may even find a real school and begin to 'work on ourselves'. The journey is long and there are many struggles along the way, but we have to persevere and keep on going. It may not be possible to see where we are going or where it is all leading, but we have to go on and trust. Find in your hearts what it means to trust. And don't give up; you can do it.

At first there is expectation, which, in this tradition, is called 'the red death'. Expectation usually leads to disappointment because our expectation comes out of our ignorance about what is needed along the Path. We may have all sorts of expectations and spiritual ambitions, which have brought us to the search in the first place, but what we are really searching for will not come about in the way that we expected. If everything were to happen just as we expected, we wouldn't need a school or a teacher because we would already know everything. We come to a real school because we are humble enough to admit a lack of knowledge and our expectations merely come from that lack of knowledge. A real school does not produce expectations. Expectation keeps us from being in

the present moment, and we can only learn in the present
moment.

We want to learn every moment of our lives, but we
can only understand a certain amount at any one time.
Sometimes we are not ready for the next step, and yet
it may seem that we are just plodding along without
really getting anywhere. It is important to remember that
even though the path can seem slow at times, or we just
don't seem to understand things the way we once did,
there is still something happening, though it may be
at a more subtle level. We may think that our time is
being wasted, but really it is not, because understanding
usually takes time. Some years later we may have a flash
of insight illuminating what, at an earlier time, we did not
comprehend. If we look at the lives of great teachers and
saints, many studied and suffered for a long time before
they were awakened.

I've had many letters from previous students who, years
later, suddenly understood what I had said to them.
You never really know when the understanding will be
granted. Maybe it will take years of various experiences to
finally come to the point when understanding is possible.
In other words, the time for you may not be ripe today,
but maybe tomorrow. The only thing we can do is to
be as awake as we possibly can in this one moment we
have. This one moment is the only time there is, and it
is not a waste of time if you're fully here. You will need
to persevere in the search until there comes the time when
you know with complete conviction what the search is for.
When the time is right you will understand what I mean.

It is inevitable that everyone on the Path goes through
what St. John called the long dark night of the soul. When
we first start the journey, having left behind the life we
knew, we are taking a step into the unknown, possibly
being guided only by our intuition and that which led
us there in the first place. There are times along the way
when it may seem very painful and confusing. We can't go
back to what we thought we were. We can't go back to our
conditioning or the life we knew before. It is like a tunnel:
in the middle we cannot see the light at the beginning or

at the end. It is here we need encouragement, guidance and understanding.

The way out is forwards. We have to keep on going until finally we do see 'the light at the end of the tunnel'. From here we can see something of the object of our search and the light acts as a guide for us to follow. Once we are in the tunnel there is really only one way out and that way is through our recognition of brotherhood and our dependence upon God. We have to hold fast to the 'rope of God' while dedicating ourselves to serving our brothers and sisters and the planet we live on. Jesus on the cross represents what we are asked to do, which is to put ourselves on the cross of sacrifice and love. The two great Commandments represent the vertical and horizontal aspects of that cross. 'Love the Lord thy God' connects us to the higher will and 'Love thy neighbour as thyself' is our reaching out to humanity. If we care about our brothers and sisters, and sacrifice ourselves to God's will, we will be led out of that tunnel. We will see the light, and we will be a light for those to come.

In our journey along the Path we can never really know exactly where we are. If we think we have 'got there', then we are inevitably in illusion because we can only see where we have been, never where we are. All we can do is rise above where we are now and see where we have been in its true context from that higher perspective. Thus, without knowing where we are, we need incredible faith with endurance and guidance. We are tested and tested at every stage, and only when we pass the tests can we move on. Like the treasure hunt, we get a clue to the next step, from which we can move on again, one clue leading to another.

Farid ud-Din Attar, the twelfth-century Sufi poet, talked about the spiritual journey towards the truth by describing it as seven valleys which are stretched out in time, though simultaneously present, because the past and the future are all here in this one eternal moment. This is an invaluable contribution to spiritual understanding, because it gives us clues to where we are, where we can go, and where we might be stuck. Each of the valleys is a goal and a trap at the same time, and within each of the valleys are guides who can lead us through it, over the mountain and to the next valley.

To go beyond a valley we invariably have to give up some of the 'baggage' onto which we hold. We have to give up more of our conditioning. The process of discarding our conditioning leads us into a new way of life and brings us closer to our freedom. On the journey we need two legs. One is our predisposition in eternity and the other is our perseverance towards the goal. We also have to question our motive along the way, making sure we are not just trying to inflate the ego. Instead, we must want to know the truth and in the process be willing to sacrifice all that we thought we were.

The first valley is the valley of quest. It is really the first initiation and is a step in an unknown direction. We enter the quest to find God, the truth, peace, oneself, or whatever, and we get very excited about it. We are brought into this quest by the 'mind' or by 'desire', neither of which can actually find the goal, but they do motivate the search. In this valley it is 'I' who searches. We assume that we know who this 'I' is but the search is for something other than 'I'. People remain in this valley for many years and sometimes their whole life. They go from one thing to another, one teacher or teaching to another, but remain trapped in the quest itself. Some are content with this valley and believe they are enlightened because of it. Eventually, however, one may come upon something that produces a very profound or loving experience.

Here we come into the valley of love, where we experience something beyond our 'I'-ness which breaks our sense of isolation and loneliness in the previous quest. We find a teacher or group or a concept of God or something that we fall in love with. We experience love for maybe the first time in our lives, and the experience is so great that we feel devoted for the rest of our lives. We think we have finally arrived at the goal. 'Love' is finally found. It is wonderful but it is also a great trap and hard to go beyond. If we can see that love is not enough, that this 'wonderful experience' is not the final goal, we might be able to come into the next valley, the valley of knowledge.

It is said that some are destined to know God and some are destined to know God and His ways. In order to be truly of service we need to know His ways, the divine laws of the universe. We need to know who we are and what we are here to do. We need the knowledge of how we can help each other and the planet as a whole. The valley of knowledge is entered when we realise we know nothing. The trap in this valley is that we try to explain it all with the mind, but the mind can only live in a world of comparison. Real knowledge is beyond comparison. It is not learned from books; it is not just more information. We come into real knowledge when we let go of our opinions and open ourselves to the truth. In this letting go of all that we think we know, we come into the valley of non-attachment. But to enter this next valley may be the hardest step of all because we have to be willing to let go of all the knowledge and all the experiences that have brought us to this point. We have to go out on our own into the unknown.

In the valley of non-attachment we are suspended with nothing to hold on to. It is potentially a time of incredible change, because in non-attachment to one's desires and concepts there is no more cohesive force to hold it all together. When there is no cohesive force, there is change. Things that we have held on to for years are released. They just fall away. Often we can feel very alone and sometimes deserted, which is the possible trap of this valley. We feel left alone because the two are moving towards the one: the division between 'you' and 'your experience' is dissolving, so there is less and less of 'you' in 'your experience'. We might even feel completely lost and fall right back into the first valley to renew the quest in some other direction. But if we remember our 'leg of perseverance' we can go through this valley and on into the valley of unity.

The valley of unity can only be entered after everything we previously thought we were has disintegrated. From the valley of non-attachment we come into a new awakening of the world. Our eyes reopen and we find that everything is One. Everywhere we turn there is One Being. In this valley we are completely here on earth. As Rumi said, 'I know that the two worlds are one'. In the valley of unity there is no real division between the 'inner' and the 'outer', and we realise that everything is becoming into the present moment. Through this realization we come into the valley of amazement.

Everything is seen exactly as it is. We are able to see the cause behind all the causes, and see the cause as its own effect. The effect is the cause of its own effect. The cause of the tree is the fruit, so the effect is really the cause. Within the fruit is the potential seed for another generation. Thus it is said that the cause of all creation is perfect man. In this valley of amazement things are seen as the becoming of being. We know there is no creation in the relative world, only the becoming of being. Here, we can really only glorify God. The danger in this stage is that we can experience God in His transcendence and forget Him in His immanence, and thus lose control of our everyday lives. That is why we need a living teacher or guide, especially in these later stages along the razor-edged path. It is essential we don't lose sight of our responsibility here on earth. Through the valley of amazement and the glorification of God, we may finally come into the valley of God-realisation.

Here we realise our complete unity with God. We realise that we have always been united with God and that the apparent separation between ourselves and the absolute was only an illusion. Here every action is God's action, every being is God's being. We have gone beyond the experience of the limited 'I'; the drop has once more been assimilated into the ocean. All illusion has passed away and there is nothing but God. Only the light of pure intelligence remains and the real Gnostic is born.

It is a long journey. It doesn't happen all at once. My teacher once gave me the following sentence to contemplate: 'Time is the eternal attribute of God.' Nothing happens too quickly, or let us say that it all unfolds in its own time. We have to learn patience and trust. We have to give ourselves up to that unfoldment of the divine plan, give ourselves up to the release of those higher energies. When the time is right in this relative world something can happen to lead us on to the next step. The laws of nature have to be obeyed. We need to respect the Way as it is given in its own time, for only then can the path to unity be followed.

4

Respect

Respect each person as a gift, just as each moment is a gift.

The awareness of God, or the knowledge of unity, does not come to us on a silver platter. We need to wake up. We need to find God in everything we see and do, then eventually we come to know that there is only One Being manifesting in different ways. So many times we think we are awake but really we are asleep, because to be fully awake would mean that we see the reality of One Being in every moment. It is not a matter of inventing a concept of God or imagining God in front of you. It is a matter of awakening to the presence of God wherever we are in the eternal now. When we are awake we cannot judge, we can only accept life exactly as it is and ourselves exactly as we are. This does not mean that there is no discrimination, because we are given the free choice to decide how to live and what to do. In fact, awareness with respect gives us the ability to see what needs to be done. But first we have to learn to respect and accept life as it is before we can do anything to serve life.

'Respect' (to see again) implies that we need to be awake in order to see the truth with a new awareness. This is the only moment that we can ever know anything or do anything. It will never be the same again and yet we are often asleep to the possibilities that lie within it. Because of our past conditioning we see the same world over and over, repeating our old habit patterns like a broken record that keeps playing the same tune. The only way to be free of this conditioning is to wake up in the moment. Do not let a moment pass without being awake; that means being awake to what is and not what we want it to be.

Respect leads us to awareness. Without respect in life we cannot be aware. When you walk about with respect, you'll respect the ground you walk on and all that you meet up with. To respect is to love God because God is the unique within the One. To respect life itself is to be grateful for God's manifestation. When we get up in the morning the pattern of the day is set by how we feel about life. If we feel miserable then everything we encounter will be miserable, and we can make others miserable as well. If they do not go along with this misery then we'll get mad that they don't agree with us and we'll be even more miserable. But if we feel grateful then we will find things to be grateful for and people will be grateful to be around us. We set the pattern of the day by the level of our vibration. And life reflects the level of our vibration.

If you could realize this you would know what it means to enter a room with respect and awareness. You would know what it means to sit down at a table with respect for the food that God has given you. You would understand why you are asked to be respectful in every moment of your lives, giving the fullest attention to whatever you are doing, whether you're sitting at a table eating, walking in a garden or making love. The future of life on this planet is in your hands. You set the pattern of the future for your children. And every time you fall asleep in denial of the great unlimited possibilities that you are, you deny the future of this planet and all that may be brought into the present moment. We are responsible for making the patterns for the future of mankind. We are responsible for laying the foundations of a new world, and this is why it is necessary to be awake.

Respect comes first, then knowledge and love. First respect the unique within the One. We need to be humble in this. Then knowledge is possible, but only through hard work. It takes time and effort to become a carpenter, a musician, a healing practitioner or anything useful in life. Knowledge requires study and practice. And then love may enter us and into our work.

Little by little we become purified as we respect the gifts and wonders we are given by God. If we consider everything as a gift of God, it is our obligation to become more and more awake, which means that we cannot allow ourselves to get caught in the 'world of attraction'. Remember to keep your intention before you at every step. You become free by learning not to identify with anything that is happening in the outer world or even in the inner worlds. You can even become free from identifying with your own state of mind, your feelings and your thoughts. But to be free does not mean that you are oblivious to the present moment. In fact, you are able to be more fully here when you do not identify with what is happening. You just need to be here totally and prepared to serve the moment in whatever way is asked.

We are here to be here, but it is rare that we are totally in our bodies, which are given to us to manifest the divine will on earth. It is about time that we appreciate our bodies and the beauty of this planet of which we are custodians. This means that we need to be awake to the present moment, which may sound simple but it is a great challenge. Our conditioned nature does not wish to be awake or manifest anything other than its own habits. Yet we know in our hearts that we are here to serve a higher purpose, so we must work on the transformation of our conditioning. The key in this is respect, because without respect we cannot be awake to the needs of the moment and the divine qualities manifesting through the moment.

Without respect we cannot know how to love one another. It is easy to see the lack of respect for the planet but it is harder to see our lack of respect for the people we know. If we all respected the people around us and the land we live upon, there would be great changes in the world. First respect, then love.

Respect each person for who they are and not what you want them to be. This is the way of love, not a struggle of personalities. In love we can only help if we respect what is real in another. We have to respect the reality of each person and then we can love. Love has nothing to do with our concepts of what that person should be or even what they think they are. It is to do with what is real; it begins with respect and this is the beginning of love. Respect comes first. This is a great key in life. We can respect ourselves and we can respect others, but we do not need to get caught up in each other's misery or lower vibrations. We might have sympathy for another's pain, but we don't need to get caught up in sentimentality which, as Rumi says, is the enemy of love.

Realize in respect that we all live in different worlds and in different times in different worlds. All the worlds are within each of us, yet some are able to move through worlds that others cannot. When we attempt to help another human being we should not manipulate them to try to experience something in the same way that we have. This can veil them from their own unique experience.

Within the One, and without denying the One, there are infinite, unique examples of the One truth and the manifestation of beauty. Love respects the differences of each creature and each reality. Love does not impose one reality upon another. Love does not attempt to convert you into something. Love completes you, it brings you into completion. What is real for you may not be real for your brother or sister. So respect the differences, but keep on reaching for the truth. Keep on reaching for the light, and use the light to focus on what is real. Finally, you may see both the infinite and the particular together in the moment. As it is said, 'Some see God in creation and some see creation in God, but a Sufi is one who sees God in creation and creation in God all in one moment.'

We all long for unity, unity within ourselves and in the world. Being in unity does not mean that we all believe in the same things or act in the same way. What it means is a knowledge of the One and the unique at the same time. The miracle of life is in its diversity. Each of us is unique. There is no one else on the face of the planet who is just like you. Nothing in the world is the same as anything else. Every thumb print and every snowflake is different from all the rest. Every being is different. Every moment is different. And yet, it is all within One Truth, One Being.

When we know this we can never again judge anything
or anyone as separate from the One truth. In our prayers
for the world or for other people we cannot judge anything.
We cannot wish for anything but their freedom, their
freedom to come into their own completion. It is not for
us to project our own opinions about what we think is
'right'. What we think is right may be right for us, but
it may not be right for another. In prayer and in love, we
can only wish for the unfolding and completion of God's
plan. We can only ask that all people come into their
own completion, their own fulfilment of their uniqueness
within the One.

To love is to care, and to care for another surely means
to accept them as unique within the One. If we are to
care for God, then we need to care for all the many living
examples of His presence. Accept the divine perfection
within each person. There is only One Absolute Truth,
which lives in the heart of each human being, whether
one knows it or not, and this truth manifests uniquely
for each human being. The body and expression of each
person is a unique manifestation of this One Truth and
a reflection of the perfect beauty of God. This is why
love begins with respect, and caring for another means
caring for that person's freedom. To care means to be
careful, to be awake and respectful. Respect each person
as a gift, just as each moment is a gift. If we really care,
then we will be awake in the moment and respect what is
given. We might not like it, but we can respect it. Where
there is respect there is the beginning of love. And when
we respect there is the possibility for learning. Without
respect we can never learn from anyone nor any moment.

To care for another means to care deeply for that person's
freedom. In order for this freedom to exist, we can ask
nothing for ourselves in that caring. If we are secretly
asking for something in return for our caring, then we
are binding that person to us. To care is to care for their
freedom. Then the caring becomes an act of service to God,
for it is God who wishes to be free. And how do we free
God? We free God by unlimiting Him from the chains of
our concepts. We free another human being in the same

way. The greatest gift we can give another human being is their freedom, the freedom to be themselves.

There is freedom only in completion. This is not a way of conversion. I would never try to convert anyone into anything. This is a complete denial of completion. The way to help someone to their completion is in recognition, the recognition of their unique nature within the unity of God. What matters is your recognition. Everyone in essence is a witness of God, the One Absolute Being. It says in the Koran, 'Wherever you look, there is the face of God.' It also says that everything shall perish except His face. What shall perish is our illusions, our illusions that there is anything or anyone other than the One Being. There is only the face of God, but the forms of appearance are different. Whoever you turn to, remember who they really are, and say to them silently inside your heart, 'Oh Thou'.

5

Learning to Love

It is our responsibility to learn how to love. By learning what love is, and its purpose, we will break through the world of illusions into the real world and we will come upon the great secret.

Love is the greatest force in the universe and the cause of all creation. We are here on this planet to learn about love, to come into the knowledge of love. And we are here to manifest this love in our daily lives. We need to realise the importance of love in our lives and the need to be conscious lovers within the Love of God. Love without knowledge is not enough. Love needs to be known and love needs to be manifested. Yet we often want to be swept away in the emotions of love without being responsible for how we love. It is our responsibility to be fully conscious in love. It is said that Love is the cause of all creation. But love is not enough, because the purpose of love is that we become conscious. It flows into the relative world as the cause of creation, but how it comes into the world is dependent upon the vehicle through which it flows. The responsibility of being human is to understand that we are here in order to be vehicles for the flow of love. We are here to know what love is and how to love.

This love is not sentimentality. In fact, it is said that sentimentality is the enemy of love. But this love is not without feeling. There is such an immensity of feeling involved that it is beyond anything normally experienced. When we open ourselves to the force of love the veils come down and the real light of understanding emerges. We have a glimpse of the real world, and in these moments we can view this world of illusion and know that if only humanity would reach out its hands in love, the power and light of love would fill the world.

A great sheikh in Turkey once said to me, 'The world is full of your prayers. Now all we need is love.' After many years I realised that for real change to come about we must know the meaning of love, of conscious love. We have to have the knowledge of love, which is the knowledge of God, since God is Love. Without this knowledge there will be no real change in the world. Yet, in man's greed and ignorance, and in his incessant search for money and power, he has forgotten the need for real knowledge. People talk about love in such a vague way that it means almost nothing. We talk about love, yet we continue to walk the streets without waking up to the real world, the world of love and the knowledge of love, of pure light and perfect order. The real world is not the chaos we see in this apparent world.

We find the real world in our responsibility in being born man and woman, that response which comes out of the greater will of God. It cannot be found from the chaos that comes out of following our little wills at the expense of the 'whole'. Ralph Waldo Emerson said, 'Woe unto him who suffers himself to be betrayed by fate.' Yet mankind accepts this fate with its ebb and flow of self-satisfaction and suffering, without any sense of obligation to the whole of life or to the future of our children's children. It is not hard to see where this has led us. It is not hard to look around and see the results of our own stupidity and greed.

Real change is necessary in our world, not just the appearance of change. But for real change to come about, the love we talk about so glibly must become conscious love. We must learn to love consciously, and that means we must know who and what we are. We have the obligation in being born man and woman to work on ourselves in order to know who we are. People say, 'I love', but do not know who this 'I' is. How can I or we say that we love, if we do not know who we are? Who is making the statement?

We do not realise that the moment we say 'I love' we bring into play a force which has its own job to do in the universe, regardless of ours, and we are lucky if we do not get hurt in the process. This force, which is the greatest force there is, comes to help us if we understand it, but it may strike us if we fail to recognise it. It is said that 'hell has no fury like a woman scorned'. A woman scorned is a woman who is not recognised for what she is, and sooner or later the frustration is liable to blow up and burst out shouting, 'Look at me! I can give you everything, yet you will not recognise me!' When we say, 'I love', that great force wishing to help us comes into play, and for a while it is possible that things will seem easy for us. But without knowledge of that force, it is liable to turn against us in its desire to be recognised.

Yet, with the mind it is not possible to know who and what we are. The mind cannot understand these things. The mind cannot understand the force of love or the knowledge of God. It is not capable of understanding unity, that God is One. The mind lives only through comparison, which is both its food and its motivation. In the real world, the world of love and order, there is no comparison, and thus no fighting, no ignorance, no disharmony. There is peace in perfect order. There is peace in knowledge. If you consider this, nothing else is satisfactory in the end. So how can we come upon this knowledge without using the mind and discursive reasoning? Is there a way to lead us ultimately to the knowledge of love and the making of a new world here on earth?

There is a way. It is the path of service and surrender. It is the path of sacrifice. To come upon the Way that leads to freedom it is necessary that we give up all the concepts of what we thought we were, or what we felt we needed in life. We have to give up all the ideas of 'self-development' or 'spiritual attaintment'. We have to break all our concepts once and for all on the stone of truth. On the path of service there is nothing to be gained for 'us', that is what we thought we were when we started the search for our true identity. There is nothing in it for this 'us' at all. We have to go on surrendering to the will of God every moment of our lives, to give up all that we considered to be real, so that little by little the illusions dissolve away and what remains is the knowledge of our essential unity with God. This is what the Sufis call *fana*, the dissolving of that which is transient, and *baqa*, the remaining of the 'permanent I' which is not separate from God.

With each moment of surrender, that which can lead us astray is redeemed into eternity, and what remains is the order that must be brought into our world. This order can lead the world out of chaos and into a new age, the second cycle of mankind, in which men and women will live upon the earth in the knowledge of the meaning of love, and become real human beings at last, God-conscious beings, awake to the real world and participating consciously in the divine plan. They will become conscious lovers, for they will know at last the meaning of love.

No, love without knowledge is not enough. We must find the knowledge beyond the mind, which bursts through us as a flash of insight, burning out the illusions in our yearning to know the truth. We are asked to come upon this knowledge, not by seeing it 'outside' somewhere or by chasing moonbeams, but by surrendering our lives totally to a life of service. Then, and only then, can we fulfil our responsibility in being born on this planet. Only then can we say in truth, 'I am'.

It is our responsibility to learn how to love. By learning what is love and its purpose, we will break through the world of illusion into the real world, and we will come upon the great secret. We are born upon this planet in order to understand love and learn to love perfectly. In this love we are fulfilling our part in the totality of God. By being able to respond to love, the cause of all creation, we are fulfilling our responsibility and purpose in this world. It is our responsibility to know our true self, which is to know the power of love coming forth into the world through us.

The true nature of our being is love and we each have the potential to love, but something often stands in the way of love. There are walls surrounding this love, keeping it from manifesting in the world. These walls need to come down before we can truly be of the Way. The walls are resentment, envy and pride, and it is these walls that prevent love from taking place. Other emotions that hold us back invariably stem from these three. If we are honest with ourselves we might see that much of what we do in life is motivated by one or more of these barriers. Resentment, envy and pride are the very denial of God and the foundation of separation. They take us out of the present moment and cause much of the pain in our lives. There is not a human being in the world who doesn't suffer from at least one aspect or more of these walls. These need to be healed because to the degree that we have any resentment, envy or pride, we are not free.

Resentment comes about from wanting to change the things we cannot change. We resent what we would like to change but cannot. We resent the past, what circumstance or other people have done to us. But we cannot change the past. We resent our parents for their rejection, for their lack of love and for their weaknesses. Yet, is it not human to have weaknesses? It is amazing how much resentment we have. In relationships the resentment may get covered up in all sorts of ways. But after a few years the resentment builds up so much that it finally blows up and the relationship with it. It is useless carrying around all this resentment. Granted, it is important to express our feelings and to stand up against injustices, but we can do this intelligently and with intention.

Most of us suffer from some sort of envy. Envy is wanting something someone else has which we do not. We want to acquire everything for ourselves. Whenever we come upon something that we do not have, we think of some reason why we should have it. If we do not envy someone else's possessions, their friends or lovers, then we might envy their experiences. Have you ever envied other people's experiences? You meet a teacher or someone who radiates love, and you envy them. You want to be just like them but you can't, because you are you and they are they. No two people from the beginning of time have ever had exactly the same experiences. God manifests differently for each person, and each person is a unique manifestation of God. Envy denies the very unfolding of God within you. To go beyond envy you have to accept yourself for who you are, and accept others for who they are.

Pride comes from feeling that we are special and that we can do it all on our own. How many people think they are special? We are each specially unique within the One, but we are not any more special than anyone else. In pride we believe that we do not need anyone else, and this actually denies God. Our pride will keep us walled in from everyone else. It has been said that no man is an island, and when you are deluded with the idea that you can do it all on your own, you should be ready for a fall. This is the meaning of the saying, 'Pride comes before a fall'. It is a fall from grace, a fall from being able to receive help. You can't do the Work on your own. You need help and you need others. If you can't accept this you will soon find yourself separated and alienated from everyone and everything, which is a very painful place to be. However, we should not revert to the other extreme, which is to feel hopeless and useless. There is nothing wrong with feeling proud when we have accomplished something. There is nothing wrong with loving oneself and feeling proud for who we are. In fact, we need to love ourselves very much and appreciate all that we are. What is important is that we recognize our dependency upon God and our interrelationship with all life.

Often, the negative emotions, such as pride, envy, resentment, apathy, grief and fear, are patterns formed in our childhood. Maybe our parents were too hard on us, or perhaps too easy. Many of our difficulties stem from the conscious or unconscious expectations of our parents. Most of us have been brought up in expectation, expected to be something or another. And this is where the illusion can begin, because the expectation imposed upon the child may stand in the way of the child's own being. Remember that a child thinks its parents are God, so what the parents believe or expect of the child becomes that child's conditioning. If we are parents we might remember this. Our children are not our own. They come to us. But it is no good blaming our parents for everything. Perhaps they were doing the best they could, and remember that perhaps they were not free of these barriers themselves.

Until we can transform the negative emotions and thought-forms of all the generations of the past, we will not be free, and we cannot free our children. As we transform the patterns of the past, so we are redeeming the generations before us. And the way to transform them is through forgiveness. As Jesus said, 'Father forgive them, they know not what they do.' All of the unredeemed thought-forms of our ancestors will continue to float about, until we learn to forgive. With every act of forgiveness we make, we are helping the conscious evolution of the planet. The transformation of these energies can only happen through conscious men and women. The transformation takes place here on earth. We can transform the negativity of the past into something useful for the future. And we have all the help we need the moment we enter the path of service.

The key to transforming these walls is through recognition. We cannot just knock these walls down with our own strength or will. The walls are thick and guarded by fierce animals, who keep us in as well as others out. The only way to bring the walls down is through recognition. The transformation of these barriers can be a great challenge. Just begin to observe yourself. The transformation occurs as we become more honest with ourselves. The moment we take courage and honestly look at ourselves, there is a possibility for the walls to dissolve. As we face the situation the way it really is, we become more and more free. Just observe yourself and see what is motivating you. What is behind your thoughts, feelings and actions? If we can look deeply at these motivators then, little by little, the walls will come crumbling down and we will be free. Love can bring these walls down. If we can learn to love and appreciate life for what it is, the walls will slowly dissolve. But we have to work at it. We have to be continually aware of our thoughts, emotions and actions, and recognise when we are holding back the flow of love in the world. To release the walls, to let them go, is a great joy, and through this we can come to know what love is.

It is possible to be in love every day of our lives. Be in love all day and every day. When you are in love you are helping the planet. You are helping very much. Whether it is in holding the hand of a child, a man or a woman, you can be in love. You can make love possible. Being grateful for being alive is making love. If life seems hard at times, you can still do it. Our life is to do with making love, and that means making love possible. This is the greatest possibility on earth. Don't waste it. Don't waste your life. This is what life is about. It's such a waste to not be in love. Only you can make love possible on earth. The whole structure of one's body changes when one is in love. The cells change. Everything changes when we are in love. This planet, this beloved earth changes when we are in love. And it can't happen without us.

However, you can't be in love unless you can forgive. How can you forgive? Simply realise that all your past has brought you to this point where you can now know the truth. Now go on. We often come into the spiritual path through pain, and it is through our own pain that we can understand others and help them through their pain. Perhaps if we had not been in pain at some time, we would never have searched for the truth. So, maybe we can even be grateful for the pain that brought us here, and give thanks to all those who have helped bring us to this one moment in time. It is said that he who thanks man thanks God. If you say thank you to somebody and mean it, you're actually saying thank you for God's grace. Live in gratefulness for all that is given.

We need to come to the place in ourselves where there is total forgiveness with no blame attached to anyone on earth for any reason. It may not be easy for some of you who have had a difficult background, but it is something you have to work on, because you cannot enter the Way without total forgiveness. It is a very important step to take. Some people have had great harm done to them in their life, and the only way to go through that pain is to forgive. It's hard to forgive when you have so much blame and so much resentment, and you want that person to pay a price for your pain. Don't live this way. Let God be the judge. What you need to do is to forgive, until there is nothing more to forgive, until it is completely over with. And the key here is to do with breath and being fully collected in the body. Find where the pain is and breathe through it with forgiveness. Do that every day until it is gone.

Forgive your parents and everyone else. In the Lord's Prayer it says, 'Forgive us our trespasses as we forgive those who trespass against us.' Our own trespasses against others, which are basically errors of ignorance, are redeemed when we forgive others. How many people do each of us carry with us from the patterns of the past? When you forgive, how many others are forgiven at the same time? A whole redemption takes place through our forgiveness, and not only will our own lives change, but the lives of others will change as well. The whole world will be affected by our forgiveness.

You will need to forgive, because you cannot be a healer without the ability to forgive first. The secret here is to sacrifice your own self-importance. Those who have difficulty forgiving are hooked on their self-importance and their self-concepts. When you stop worrying about yourself so much, then forgiveness is easier. So sacrifice into forgiveness. Sacrifice the self-concepts and the self-importance, then it's all much easier. If you can make that sacrifice, then you will know forgiveness. With forgiveness comes divine compassion and the glorification of all life. Then you may finally come into total amazement, thus beginning to understand the miracle of life itself.

6

Recognition

We can bring forth the beauty in each other by recognising the beauty in each other.

It is said that we are dependent upon the rain from heaven. This is the grace which descends upon the world and fills the world. There is a divine music filling the space of this world. It is the music of the spheres, and we can only hear it from the inner ear of the heart. We can open to it and let it fill our souls. It can transform our lower nature and lift us into higher realms of life. From the beginning of time mystics have attempted to attune themselves to this formative sound, this music of the spheres. In the love for this sound, many have expressed what they have heard through music and art. Sound creates pattern. Many of the great architects have seen this geometry of the formative world and used it in their work throughout history. Deep inside our soul we yearn to recognise this music, this pure geometry of life and beauty, because the heart of the universe is within us and it seeks to unfold through us.

We need to attune ourselves to the purest note and live at the most perfect pitch, so that we may become the everlasting example of divine truth. We then become the expression of the divine heard in the music of the spheres. We are the instruments of God, as in the saying of Rumi, 'I am the flute, but the music is thine.' Obviously, the instrument needs to be finely tuned. The first step is to be in a receptive state in order to hear the uniquely perfect note that lies within ourselves. We can open ourselves and allow ourselves to be changed, to be tuned by the love of

God. Allow yourselves to be seen, to be heard and to be loved.

The angels are like harmonics of the one pure light from which all things come. The angels respond as harmonics whenever a pure note is sounded. Our responsibility is to strike that first pure note, and then every bit of help we need will be given to us. It is the quality of the note we strike that determines the harmonics returning to us. Any note produced, whether we are awake or not, will have harmonic effects. If the note is confused or based upon something of our lower nature, then what comes back is of a similar vibration. If we can strike a pure and beautiful note, then the angels will sing at our feet.

Listen to the sounds of the world around you. Listen to the sounds unheard by the average ear. You may hear the sounds of the potter's wheel and his hands shaping the clay, but can you also hear the sound of his intention? And can you hear the sounds of the bowl, containing the emotions and thoughts of the potter at the time of its creation? There is a difference between one bowl and another, even though they appear to be the same. The difference is in the sounds crystallised within them. If we listen very carefully we can hear the moment speak, for each moment has a sound and something to tell us. There is a language of the moment and a message of the moment.

There is a sound to everything. There are the heavy sounds, like grief and depression, and there are lighter sounds, like joy and humour. There are sounds that can uplift us beyond the narrow boundaries of our pre-conceived notions, and sounds that can sweep the imagination into higher realms of infinite possibility. Sound and thought fix the pattern of our lives. We are either free in the beauty of the moment for what it is, or we are trapped in the ugliness of our judgement. If we are in judgement, then that is the sound we convey.

Let us be aware of the tone of our voice. If we are full of judgement, resentment, envy or pride, the tone of our voice will reflect this and it will be heard on some level. Children especially are aware of the voice and it has an effect upon them. The sound of the truth is found between the words. The tone comes through. More and more I come to understand the importance of tone, because I speak with so many different kinds of people. The tone of my voice can carry the intention of my heart. What is the tone of your prayers? What is the tone of your life? What is the sound that carries from you? Maybe we can find the sound of love and attune ourselves to this, then others will hear and know what that sound is.

As we develop our sensitivity we can start to hear these inner sounds. The sound of gratefulness can pass from one person to another faster than the opening and closing of an eye. Laughter can be the same. Whenever there is the sound of gratefulness there is no resentment or bad feelings. There can be no judgement. Gratefulness melts all other sounds within it. We cannot hear it by trying too hard. We can only open ourselves to it. It is always here. It is not a matter of being grateful because it is a beautiful day and things are going so well. What if things aren't going so well? Can we still hear the sound of gratefulness? It is not dependent upon what we like or don't like, because this involves comparison of opposites. This is a state of duality and it is important that we remember to live in unity. The mind or our memory patterns will take us from one extreme to the other. The mind is happy when the sun is out but when the fog rolls in it gets upset. The ordinary mind lives in duality. Only the heart can hear the true sound of gratefulness. It takes work to be grateful all the time. It is not easy but we can learn to be grateful, no matter what is happening in the moment. It is one of the greatest secrets in life. Let the sound of gratefulness resonate in your hearts.

What appears in this world are opposites such as man and woman, sun and moon, life and death. It is only through direct perception from the heart that one can actually see both at once, in unity, and that perception is a gift of grace. The goal of any real teacher is to bring us to unity, and within this unity we can see the opposites and the multiplicity. There has to be multiplicity in order for there to be a world. There also has to be a creative tension between opposites and between the affirming and denying forces, otherwise there would be no experiment of life on earth. Thus duality exists, but the sound of gratefulness is not in duality. It is in unity.

If we can see the world as it really is, we then see the perfect patterns behind it. We can look at a daisy and see its underlying proportion and pattern. We can see this if we are awake. When we are grateful we can see. The flowers come alive. Everything comes alive: the patterns, the colours, the textures, everything, when we are grateful. How does this happen? Mevlana said, 'It is light that makes colour visible.' When we are grateful, light fills our hearts and we are able to see the world as it truly is, the wonder that it truly is. Love fills our hearts. Perhaps one day we will be in love all the time; what a possibility. Well, we can, we all can be in love. Then, wherever we stand is holy ground.

How often do we recognise the beauty of life? There is so much beauty around us, so many miracles of God, and yet we walk around asleep to the wonders of life. Awareness is something we have to work on. We have to open ourselves consciously to the beauty around us. Listen to the effect inside yourselves. Feel what it is, without judging or comparing it to something else. Open up your senses and sensitivities. Reverse space.

There are two sorts of space. One we have termed centric space, which is what most of us live in ninety-nine percent of the time. It is like a dot in the middle of a circle saying 'I see', 'I hear' or 'I'm doing'. It is the sense of approaching everything around us with this ego-centric 'I'. In this space we are not really listening, but think that we are. Actually, we are talking and not listening; we are too much in the way to really hear.

The other sort of space is the reverse of this, and could be called peripheral space, or reversed space. It is like a circle spiralling into the centre. Instead of reaching out to grab what we want in the world, or seeing only what we want to see, we allow the impressions of the world to come to us. It is being receptive, being actively receptive. We allow the world to speak and move through us. We allow life to see and penetrate us. We are not the central focus. Here, we need to surrender ourselves to the space coming in, becoming empty of self, so that the life around us can be heard. We need to become quiet and receptive. Then we can hear. Instead of 'I hear' or 'I see', it is 'I am heard', 'I am seen'. Once we realise we are heard, then we can truly hear. If we can allow ourselves to be seen, we will be able to see, and hopefully some day we will see that we are loved.

To understand what I mean by this I suggest you go out and allow yourselves to be seen. Allow yourselves to be seen by the trees, the plants, the animals, the land. Go out and about, and let the land see you. If the land has been raped, you'll feel its pain. Consider what the birds feel, the trees, the land. The moment you allow yourselves to be seen you'll start to really see what's there. Things will begin to happen. It sounds so simple, but the effect can be quite tremendous and far reaching. By reversing space we ourselves become the mirror for life to know itself. You'll be able to see and understand all the kingdoms, including the invisible ones, when you allow them to see you.

We are the eyes through which God sees, the ears through which He hears, the nose through which He smells, the hands through which He touches, and the mouth through which He speaks. We can come to realise God in every moment of our lives, and in this knowledge we are in love. The truth and beauty of God are no more 'inside' or 'outside'. They are beyond any such division, because we are aware of God inside and outside simultaneously. 'Some see God in creation and some see creation in God, but the Sufi sees God in creation and creation in God all at the same time.'

Begin to be aware of and open yourselves to the beauty that surrounds you. We can bring forth the beauty in each other by recognising the beauty in each other. It is said, 'Beauty is in the eye of the beholder,' and there is a key in this. The sole purpose of love is beauty, and love finds the beloved in the beautiful. In love we can recognise the beautiful and bring forth the latent beauty in all things.

Unfortunately, we may get caught in the world of comparison and judge everything according to our scale of beauty. Can we say that one note is more beautiful than another, when each plays a part in the overall music? Look at how other cultures see beauty in different ways, dress in different ways, sing in different ways and design their lives in different ways. Are we right and they wrong? It is often difficult to see beyond our own conditioning and see how other people behold the world. But can we learn to relax our judgements and begin to respect all life, and then we may begin to recognise the beauty in each other.

When we recognise the essence of life in, let us say, a tree, then that tree comes alive. When we give recognition to the land it sings for us. The world around us has much to give if only we would recognise it. The planet needs to be recognised for all that it gives us. When we recognise and cooperate with the invisible kingdoms, without which nothing may come to pass, they cooperate with us in what we need to do. All of life and all the elements of this planet are crying out, 'Recognise us and we can help you.'

With the knowledge of breath the elements can be our friends. It is not a forced friendship. It is a friendship out of love and recognition. Man and the elements will some day work together and this will be the beginning of something very wonderful for the planet. The secret is in the power of breath and our love through recognition.

Through recognition we can serve the planet. The conscious man can say, 'I am' and 'I will', because he knows himself and knows that it is through him that all things return to their source. It is through conscious man that the kingdoms on earth return to their source. It is through our recognition that all life may come to know it is loved. This recognition is not just of the 'outer' form of life, however beautiful, but it is a recognition of the 'inner' essence and qualities present within the form, be it a rock, plant, animal or human being.

The trees and animals do not yet know that we can recognise their inner qualities because we have not yet done so. Do the various aspects of your own body, emotions and mind know that they are recognised? So many of the struggles and wars upon the planet, and within ourselves, have been caused by the feelings of isolation and separateness from unity. We clash and struggle with each other, while ignoring the divine aspects of each other. A lot of unnecessary pain is caused by a lack of recognition of the inner value of other people or of life.

In reality there is nobody we have not met before. This is a very bold statement that cannot be understood with the mind. It is a great understanding if we can come to grips with it. We may not know each other's personalities, but in reality we have known each other. We can recognise each other in this way. Every human being in the world wishes to be known. Every child wants to be recognised. When we recognise a child we honour the freedom of that being to grow up in love.

A joyous state unfolds when we realise that we already know each other. We know each other in a very deep way. If we can see this we'll be able to relax and open up more with each other. We can trust the moment and come into a knowledge of love together. To love each other in the name of God means that we are not separate from each other, but are each unique examples of the unity.

When we can be together in love something great is released in the world. The whole world is right here, and if we can sit together in love, which is prayer, then something glorious is occurring in the world at the moment. This is the power of love. It is a conscious love, a love in knowledge. To come together in this infinite possibility of ourselves in the recognition of knowing one another without the form is a great joy. It is the beginning of real love. Once we take a step into this way of love we are not alone. Every human being longs to be in this way, by whatever name they might call it, because every human being wishes and longs for the freedom of knowing that they are loved.

7

Breath

*The breath is possibly the deepest mystery of all things in
this life.*

The secret of life is in the breath. We come into this world
on the breath and we go out on the breath, but if we are
not awake to breath we will surely die asleep to the reality
of life itself. Breath is life. Without it there is no life. But
we presume breath, just as we presume life. It happens,
and we just go on living unconsciously, until finally we
are presented with death and wonder what happened to
life. Unless we are conscious in breath, we are asleep to
life. The average man, living his life in a mechanical way,
forgets all about breathing until the moment of his death,
when he struggles to draw the last breath, clutching to the
remnants of what he has known as life. It is so easy to take
breath for granted but it is really an obligation in our lives
to learn how to breathe consciously. If we are living life
passionately and really love being here, we will want to
explore the depths of this great miracle.

The spiritual world is right here, in life. It *is* life. And
we cannot be here, we cannot even be alive, without
breath. Few people can accept the responsibility of being
alive, which is to inhabit this body and be custodians of
this planet. This requires tremendous respect. We are not
just our bodies, our emotions or our thoughts, but we must
totally inhabit the vehicles we have been given, through
which we can express the Spirit of life. That is what it is
all about. And the secret to this is in the breath. In many
languages 'spirit' and 'breath' come from the same root
word. The Spirit of life is carried on the breath. To be

conscious of life we must be awake to the breath. In fact, it is not even possible to be conscious, in the true sense of that word, without being awake to the breath.

Can you make love consciously without being awake to the breath? Can you prepare food consciously, being awake to the life within the food, without being aware of the breath? Everything is within the breath or, as it was put by Ibn 'Arabi, another of the great Sufi mystics of the thirteenth century, 'All is contained in the divine breath like the day in the morning's dawn.' You can breathe in any colour you want, any element or vibration, from anywhere in the world, without leaving the room. It is all possible. It is not difficult and just takes practice. Healing is carried through the breath, telepathy is carried through the breath and the transmission of *baraka*, spiritual grace, is carried through the breath. Think of the wind. It blows and carries with it whatever is light enough to be lifted from the earth. It carries the scent of flowers. It carries the leaves as they fall from the trees. It carries the seeds from the plants to where they may take root.

The possibilities lying within the understanding of breath are enormous and the greatest challenge is to be continually awake within it. Can we learn to breathe with life? Can we learn to breathe with God? To breathe with God we need to surrender to God or, as Mevlana said, 'If you want to live, die in love; die in love if you want to remain alive.' This is the passion of surrender that we need in order to reach union with God. It is surrender, not achievement. There is nothing for you to achieve. There is only One Absolute Being unfolding from the essence of itself into every single moment and through every single being, and it all happens through the breath.

The awareness of breath is necessary every day, every moment. We can begin by watching the rise and fall of the breath. This itself takes much practice, and few people are prepared to make the necessary effort. When we can just watch the breath we will start to realize that we are continuously being tyrannised by thoughts that move us this way and that. Although we do not like to face the truth, it may become clear to us that we have little permanence. What we think 'we' are is constantly changing. We might realize that we are not our thoughts, any more than we are our emotions or our bodies. Why do we find it so difficult to watch the breath without being moved all over the place by thoughts? Until we learn to breathe consciously and develop a permanent 'I', or 'observer', we can always be led astray. Only when we learn to breathe in awareness can there be a chance to come upon the inner being that is our real self.

Unless we are 'on top of' the breath, in awareness, we cannot hear; we cannot even begin to know of our inner being because we are still involved with our lower nature and the chattering of the mind. Unless we are on top of the breath we cannot begin to be of service because we are not really here in the present moment. When we are on top of the breath we have the possibility to give something to the world and the future to come. We are here to give, to give all of ourselves, in total commitment to life. This is what we are asked to do in return for the gift of life that has been given to us. It is useless to talk about 'self-development' or even 'self-fulfilment' if we cannot breathe out consciously with love and compassion.

Without conscious breath there can be no flow of life energy. The energy of life is all around us and we can consciously bring it into us for our use and then give it back in service. A teacher of mine once gave me the instruction, 'Breathe in only to breathe out.' Eventually there ceased to be any sense that I was breathing; I was being breathed. This can only happen when the in-breath and the out-breath are balanced, which means that we are in harmony with the divine flow of life. In harmony we have the possibility to help one another.

The breath is possibly the deepest mystery of all things in this life. Everything is contained within the breath. All life is available to us through breath, so, as we breathe in, we can breathe anything we need, from any place in the universe. And as we breathe out, we can give something of ourselves back to life, helping create a pattern for the world to come. Our breath is not limited by walls. We can breathe in from all directions, consciously breathing in what God gives us, and breathe out to anywhere it is needed. We can even choose the quality of our breath, and that quality depends upon our degree of awareness. Remember that there is one thing we all share and that is air. We are a cosmic apparatus for the transformation of subtle energies, but without the breath there can be no transformation. There can be no purification of life without the breath.

People do not realise that something is being born out of every moment, and that if we could find the right rhythm of breath that is most natural and most in harmony with the universal laws governing our existence, we would have the possibility of contributing to the work of bringing about peace on this planet. Through the breath we can be of service to life by coming into harmony with it.

There is a breath of the womb of the moment. It is the breath of the matrix of life. Like the physical womb of the mother, it contains the matrix of possibility for life on earth. The present moment 'pulsates', expanding and contracting, coming into existence and passing out of it instantaneously. Everything is born from this rhythmic pulsation of the womb of the moment. This rhythm also produces the waves of vibration that make up the subtle or formative worlds interpenetrating this physical world of form. All of these worlds interpenetrate each other, each with different rates of vibration. Everything depends upon the rate of vibration, just as sound creates pattern and pattern creates form. We can tune into the higher rates of vibration through the refined quality of our breath. There is infinite possibility lying in the 'here and now'. Within this breath, which I call the mother's breath, is the whole octave of life. With every act of love we make, with every conscious breath we take, a child is being born—maybe not a physical child but a real child nonetheless. This is a great responsibility, that we can bring forth something new into the world through our love and through our breath, in every moment of our lives.

8

Consciousness

It is said that man, meaning man and woman, is the manifested consciousness of God.

Most of us think we are conscious when in fact we are asleep. To be conscious requires effort, and we cannot be conscious without being conscious of the breath. People sometimes misuse the word 'consciousness' and say they are expanding 'their' consciousness. But consciousness is not something you can own or expand. There is no 'your' consciousness and 'my' consciousness. You might be conscious of something different than I am, but the energy of consciousness is the same. To be conscious implies that we are awake, and although there are different levels or degrees of being awake, the fundamental reality of consciousness is the same everywhere. It is an energy that we can come into. It is a possibility for the human being, but we must never presume that we are conscious.

If you are not conscious then you cannot say that you have consciousness, let alone expand it. When people say that they are expanding consciousness they are usually expanding their concepts of themselves into a world of their imagination. Consciousness is not something that you can develop. You can come into it, but you cannot develop something that you do not already have. Generally people have some degree of sensitivity, as well as a lot of thoughts and emotional habits, but consciousness is of a higher order of existence. It is an energy that you can come into but only if you are free of the illusions of the conditioned mind. It is beyond concepts and beyond sensitivity; it is even beyond mind. Yet it is through this energy of consciousness that the creative energy, coming from the higher worlds, can unfold in the world.

I can help you see certain things but I cannot make you conscious. To become conscious is up to you. You cannot expect anybody else to be conscious for you. This may appear to be obvious, but we often walk around asleep, expecting other people to be awake to what is needed. It is a sort of unconscious expectation that other people will take care of you, take care of the house or take care of the world. No, you have to wake up, and the way to begin is to be here right now, in your body, in the space around you, in this moment. This is the beginning of consciousness. It is being who you are and knowing where you are at the same time. And for each person that is different. There's no sense in trying to copy somebody else. How are you going to copy my consciousness? How are you going to copy my experiences? You can not.

We need to be careful not to presume that our ordinary consciousness, or our level of attained consciousness, is the highest possible or the only mode of experience. This assumption would limit us. We need to consider the possibility that there are higher levels or worlds beyond our ordinary level of consciousness. If we do not limit ourselves to any one level, then immense possibilities open up for the personal consciousness to be integrated into higher levels of understanding.

These levels, or worlds, interpenetrate our own and can be of use if we open ourselves up to work with them, for they do wish to work with us. Yet we must remember that this integration is only possible when we are fully here, in our bodies and in this world. Then transformation is really possible, not only the transformation of energies within us, but also the possible transformation of other people and the space around us.

The world of our senses, and even the higher worlds unknown by the senses, are not outside us. In one way the world is outside us and we relate to it, but we can know the world from within, as well as from without. Our degree of consciousness is the bridge between the world governed by the senses and the higher worlds. This is also true of the world of ideas. Ideas may seem to come to us from outside ourselves, but they are really known from within. We have an innate notion of the truth, which attracts the truth from the world outside. This is part of the law, 'Like attracts like'. The soul is a knowing substance, and this means that there is something innate within us that recognizes the truth in the world around us. So, while knowledge is developed through experience in this world, it does not really come from without but it is a recognition from within. The soul recognizes the idea from within the impressions of this world around us.

As a simple example, all chairs come from the idea of 'chairness', of what a chair is and does. We can recognize this idea within the physical form of the chair. We can see the whole process of making the chair and the idea from which it came. We might consider the wood used for building the chair, the sacrifice of the tree, the process of design, the planning, cutting, fitting, gluing, and all the necessary things involved in its construction. If we reverse time, as it were, we can return through the creation process of the chair to its source. According to a Sufi saying, 'There is no creation in the relative world, only the becoming of being.'

This way of remembering the source in the creation of anything or in any impression we receive can lead us into the realization that there is nothing outside of our being, since there is nothing outside the One Being. Most of the time, being governed by our senses, reality is seen to be outside ourselves. If we could receive impressions consciously, which means having a 'permanent observer' to recognize the impressions as coming from the One Source of all life, then we would experience the world in a new way and be able to digest the impressions as food for our being.

The secret here is to observe the world as emerging from One Being, for there is really only One Being manifesting in different ways. The observer is impartial and not attached to the senses. It does not make judgements or comparisons about events, but simply observes and assimilates the impressions for what they are. Comparison is the food of the mind; the observer does not need comparison. It is perfectly possible to live life passionately, but not be controlled by the passions. In this way, as we feel more and know more of reality, we see the world for what it is rather than what it just appears to be.

It is said that the Sufi is in this world but not of it. This is a world of appearances, which is at the same time a mirror of higher worlds. The world we know is a relative world of time and space where opposites and differences exist. The actual beauty of this world is because of these differences and in how the opposites are harmonized through man and woman. If there were no differences or diversity there would be no art, no music and no life. This world requires the creative tension of opposites, and it is here we can see the miracle of multiplicity. Unity is not the miracle; the miracle is in the diversity.

Ultimately everything comes from the absolute and is a division from the unity, without which there would be no creation. As it is said in the Tao Te Ching, 'The One creates the two, the two creates the three and from the three come ten thousand things.' The first split into two represents the difference between God and Man. It is the difference between the absolute and the relative. We are the necessary reflection of God in the relative world, as is written in the Bible, 'God created man in His image'. In man are all of the worlds, and it is said in the Koran, "The worlds are not big enough to contain Me, but the heart of My faithful servant can contain Me."'

The universe was made for man and woman and not the other way around. There is no creation in the relative world. There is only the becoming of being. Remember that everything is happening at once but it takes time to unfold. There is only One Absolute Being from which all becomes, as it is written in the Koran, 'He said be, and all became.' We are the links between heaven and earth. Being becomes through man and woman. We are the manifested consciousness of God.

Consciousness is the reaction of active intelligence to pattern. What we are involved with is pattern, whether it is the pattern of healing or the pattern of thought-form. We need awakened intelligence which gives us the ability to recognize pattern. The whole secret of creation is within the knowledge of the hierarchy of God's qualities emanating from the One Source of all life. Pattern literally comes from that source into colour, sound and form. To recognize this, we need active intelligence which requires will and complete wakefulness. It has nothing to do with 'going into a trance'. It is being completely awake to the patterns of life, awake to the shapes and forms coming into manifestation. Learn to be conscious of the most perfect patterns in nature and in life, which emanate from the most perfect names of God, the divine archetypes, and to which we are asked to serve. There is perfect beauty all around us, but without consciousness and without active intelligence to serve it, it is wasted, unseen and unused.

Through recognition, active intelligence gives life to form. If you listen to music or watch birds fly homeward, you can see the pattern coming into form. When we wake up to pattern, we see that each sound, each pattern, each shape is for a different purpose. When we hear a particular piece of music, or hear the waves break on the sand, or hear a baby cry in the night, something happens inside us. There is a particular reaction, which is more or less conscious and dependent upon our degree of intelligence recognizing and reacting to that pattern. The soul is, in a sense, made up of music and we all could hear that music as we meet soul to soul.

We are asked to act in this world with intelligence. First there is pattern. Then there needs to be the intelligence to see it and bring it into being. This can be related to anything you do in your life. What is the pattern of your actions, or the pattern of your decisions? There is a pattern to every decision and to every action. What is the pattern of your life? There is the chaotic pattern that holds us back from our potential intelligence, and there is the deeper pattern that is contained within the divine essence, which can only come forth through the active intelligence of consciousness. It is up to us which pattern we choose. It is quite a responsibility to realize that pattern is created through us. We are setting the pattern of the world to come through the pattern of our lives.

9

Divine Order

The divine order yearns to manifest on earth and it is up to us to be the vehicles for this.

There is a divine order within and manifesting through life. This can be called the 'real world'. It can be known, but you have to go beyond form and see the patterns behind the world of appearances. It is a formative world, a world of perfect pattern, which shapes all life. It is not an arbitrary thing.

Science has proved that certain patterns and proportions form the structure of all living things. There is a perfect order at the basis of life. It has been used in sacred architecture throughout history to bring forth the possibility of a harmonious pattern on the land and in our lives. We can put into use these sacred proportions, which can then reflect the divine order.

This world is a reflection of the real. In the Hermetic tradition it is said, 'As above, so below'. As human beings, we are asked to participate consciously in this work of transformation, for without us it cannot be fulfilled. We are asked to come into harmony with the divine order, surrendering our hearts to it, and thereby bringing about the possibility of the perfection of God on earth.

The perfection of God can be made manifest on earth according to the degree of our knowledge and our capacity to bring it forth. The Sufis say, 'Only God is perfect', but still we can strive for perfection and help bring it forth to a greater degree. It is a question of continual refinement. Each day we can surrender to this unfolding, allowing ourselves to be an ever-greater vehicle for this truth. If we can align ourselves to this divine principle we can help serve the Work which is so needed in the world today.

Unfortunately, the world seems to be moving towards disorder and chaos. It is moving away from divine order. If we choose not to live in this chaos, and instead attune ourselves to become more in harmony with the divine, then we can be the instruments for the return of mankind to order. It is up to each of us to wake up to our responsibility. If we are not awake and turning toward the truth at all times, then we will be swayed here and there into the disorder of the world around us. If we can be awake and live in harmony with the divine order, then we can help bring forth a new world.

Man needs to discover his true identity so that he can finally say with complete conviction, 'I Am'. As G.I. Gurdjieff said, 'Life is real only when I Am.' We make life real by being real ourselves, by knowing ourselves and fulfilling what we are meant to do. Love can only flow into the relative world through conscious man. Remember the words in the Lord's Prayer, 'Let Thy kingdom come, Thy will be done, on earth as it is in Heaven.' The world of possibilities within the essence of God needs to manifest into the relative world. The divine order yearns to come on earth, and it is up to us to be the vehicles for this.

God needs man. God's will, which is perfect order, can only be brought into manifestation through man, meaning man and woman. When we know there is a divine order we can begin to pray and work within this; we can begin to trust in it. We can set an intention 'outside of time' for the divine order to manifest through us. Our lives can be fully dedicated to a life of service. It is not a question of serving to get something in return. Service is not like this. Rather, there is no other intention but to serve unconditionally, and this is a beautiful way to live. Every time we dedicate ourselves to life from 'outside of time', we help bring the divine order into time. From the moment our feet first touch the ground in the morning, every step we take can be in the remembrance of God, with the intention of serving life unconditionally.

It is possible to live consciously in the divine order and manifest it in each and every moment. We manifest the perfection when we are in perfect flow with it. Order is usually thought of as something strict and rigid, but it is not like this. Order is actually perfect flow. It is not rigid at all, but it is pure and adaptable like water. When we are empty to the concept of ourselves as separate from the whole and committed to a life of service, then we can be in the flow, wherein lies true freedom.

Throughout time the concept of 'perfect man', sometimes called completed or universal man, has existed. The perfect man is the one who has knowledge of the perfection of God, who sees the divine order in all things. The vastness of the universe is contained within the heart of perfect man, who is the bridge between time and eternity.

The perfect man sees God in creation and creation in God at the same time. Thus he is actually necessary for the unfoldment of the divine order and the fulfilment of the experiment of life on earth. This is a secret which we must decipher. The universe was created for perfect man, who is actually the cause of all creation. The roots may appear to be the cause of the tree, but in reality the roots and the whole tree came into existence for the sake of the fruit. Just as the fruit is the cause of the tree, perfect man is the cause of what we call creative evolution.

There is a contemplation, 'What were you when you were just a thought in the mind of God at the beginning of creation?' We were complete. You see, we were already complete in the mind of God before anything ever happened. Now we have the possibility of coming into our own completion. We are coming into being but it takes time in this world, just as a vision takes time to manifest. The cause of our existence and the whole evolutionary scheme of things is for the fulfilment of that perfect idea in the mind of God. A real esoteric school is one that helps in the preparation of this fulfilment.

What is perfect man? There is a saying, 'The believer has a heart but the Gnostic has no heart.' The heart of perfected man is the home of truth. Truth can only live in the heart, and anything, any beliefs whatsoever, can fill up that space and prevent the ultimate truth from unfolding. An empty centre is created as we turn back towards truth, and the more we turn the more we come towards our own completion. We turn inside straight to God, trusting that which we can never completely know, but which can only know itself in us.

To trust in God means that we trust in love, because God is love. As Ibn 'Arabi said, 'The ultimate goal of love is to know the reality of Love and that reality of love is identical with the essence of God.' Divine love is not just an abstract quality. It is the essence of life. In divine love there is no particular object involved, no state of duality. There is nothing other than this divine love. There is only One God and there is only one love. It is not one person loving another as someone separate, but each person recognising the love that exists between them. It is God loving Himself in us. All manifestations of love are from this One Divine Love. The purpose of love is beauty and God loves the beautiful in us. All beauty comes out of divine love, and love is the cause of all creation and the cause of our return.

In essence everything is complete. This is a tremendous realisation if you can accept it. If you can really take it into your heart, your whole life will change. In this completion is the matrix of all life. A key to understanding the completion is in the Virgin Mary. It is said that ever since the time of the Virgin Mary there is no more need to think. This is because the matrix is already complete. You can't understand this with the linear mind. You have to go beyond your thoughts about time and understand it in your heart. The completion already exists. The matrix of life is in essence perfect.

The matrix contains perfect pattern and geometry, from which all possibilities exist. It is like a womb from which all things come into being. It exists in eternity, and so it is always existent in the present moment, the only moment there is. Within the present moment is the womb of possibility. A Sufi is sometimes called the son of the moment, because he is continually dying and being reborn in each moment. Remember, the womb is complete in itself. It is perfect and all things come out from it. The matrix of life is already complete. We do not need to make it, we just need to fulfil it. We are asked to surrender ourselves to this perfection already within life, and then dedicate ourselves to serving it every moment of our lives.

Active love, which is service, can come about when we know something about the matrix. Acting out of love has to do with being in the fire of love. Mevlana said, 'I want only burning, burning,' and that burning in the heart brings forth the matrix into manifestation. That burning in the heart will go on until there is only love.

The essence of the matrix within all of us is perfectly complete, but it is for man to recognise the perfection in woman, and through this he will come into the knowledge of the perfection of God. Woman is essentially born complete, but man has to learn completion. The woman in man is fragile, but the man in woman is not. The woman is fragile because she needs to be recognised; woman is freed through recognition. Man must recognise the completion that he may become complete, and to be complete is to know love. First we must recognise the perfect matrix, and then we can learn to serve it.

I was told that there are two possible ways on the road of life. One is the gentle way of Mary, and the other can be called the terror of Christ. Of course, there are different levels of meaning in this. If only we could relax into what we have to do, which is to surrender to the matrix in the gentle way of Mary, then it would be an easier, gentler transition. But so often we resist facing the necessity of real change.

We recognise the earth as a living matrix yet look at what is happening to the land, to the water, to the air, to the biosphere. Forests are being destroyed, soils are being depleted, even the oceans are being saturated with pollutants. Once we can recognise the divine perfection right here on earth, then we can help bring forth that latent potential within the matrix of life. To have faith in the essential perfection of life is to realise our own responsibility in this. Within this faith we cannot sit back and expect God to complete the Work for us. Remember, God needs man; we are the hope of the world. All hope for the Kingdom of God on earth is in our hands and this hope is dependent upon our response to the divine order, the manifestation of God's will on earth.

10

Time and the Octave

God makes the seasons, but man makes time.

Real action does not come from this world, which we call the world of appearances, but from a world beyond. It must come across a bridge between this world and the world to come. This is the secret of time and action. Time and action are made through us. Time is not an arbitrary thing floating on in a linear way; we make it happen. We do it in consciousness. We make time by agreement. We can bring the world to come, which in essence is perfect like the matrix, into this moment. An immense possibility exists and it is up to us to make order out of it. To create a new and perfect order is to disintegrate old concepts of ourselves and life, leading us to greater freedom, greater space and greater realisation about the purpose of our being born. If you were a sculptor, for example, you would take clay, which has all the possibility within it for the work at hand, and you would create order from it. You would shape it into something, creating space, time and dimension out of its given potential.

Time is something that many people either ignore or presume. How often do we really consider the time we have, the time we are given in this life, on this planet? To presume time is to let time pass away, and that is a waste of time. It is a question of what we do with time. Some people need to see time, some need to go through time and some need to manifest time. To see time is to understand it. To go through time is to redeem the past by allowing the future to come in. To manifest time is to create time in order to do something with it. God makes the seasons but man makes time. We create time; time is in our hands.

To manifest time is to manifest energy. Energy is all around us and it is up to us to bring it into something, into time. We can do something useful with this time rather than wasting it, for ourselves, our children and our children's children. To waste time is to waste our lives, and since our lives are a gift given to us, we are also wasting God's time.

Our job, as human beings, is to participate in the manifestation of God's will on earth. First we need the knowledge of how to do this and then we need to be willing to fulfil our unique function. We can see how this works in the manifestation of an idea. First there is the idea and then there is the feeling or desire to express it. Finally there is the expression. A whole process must take place in time for an idea, from the world of possibility, to manifest. It takes time and it takes work, and the more we know about the laws of time and manifestation, the better we can serve that expression.

There needs to be an intention and sufficient energy directed properly to see an idea through to its completion. We also need to be willing to do it. For there to be a flow from the world of archetypes into manifestation it is necessary that we give our agreement and assistance to the process by saying, 'I will'. We need commitment and agreement, and also perseverance to fulfil the task. Whenever we consciously affirm 'I will' to an aspect of the divine plan, we are given exactly what we need to fulfil that plan. There needs to be the triad of commitment, willingness and agreement. I call this the 'triad of freedom'. Through this triad of freedom we are placed in the stream of service and can thus participate in the manifestation of being into becoming.

We have to really desire to manifest God's will to the best of our abilities. Without this we will never put in all of our effort. It is important to visualise whatever we are asked to do with our deepest feelings and the desire to complete it. We cannot expect that it will all happen easily, or even complete itself in the way that we envision.

We can only do our best and pray that it will work out in the best way possible. There is no need to feel attached, but it is good to care very deeply. Then from the feeling and thought there needs to be action, because without action there can be no manifestation in this world.

The definition of patience is the distance between vision and manifestation. If we are impatient we will not give enough time for a vision to manifest. Patience is active, not passive. We need to work at it. It is an actively receptive state because we need to wait for the right time, taking care not to fall asleep and miss it.

As human beings we have to make decisions and follow them to their destination if we are to get anywhere in life. Often we are diverted by accident and fate. Who is in control if we are not awake and do not make conscious decisions? We cannot expect God to make our decisions for us, though we can ask for guidance; we cannot expect God to do what needs to be done in order to reach the destination; we cannot expect God to make it all happen. We have to make the effort ourselves; *we* have to make the decision.

Normally we start off with good intentions, but things rarely get completed. We need sufficient energy and sufficient will to complete things. Although we make an intention and begin, there are places in its fulfilment where we have the tendency to divert the intention or fall asleep and so need extra effort to keep the flow going. We can, in fact, completely forget the original intention, for hours, for days, for years or for a lifetime. It is the knowledge and practice of the laws of time that can help us to fulfil our task.

There are two sorts of time. One is the natural time based upon the seasons and night and day. The other is the time that is created by a human being who knows how to use time. Without this knowledge of time there can be no real change. We only repeat, in different ways, the habit patterns of our conditioning. We have to understand the laws that govern our existence and abide by them. Time is cyclical and repetitive until we learn how to use the laws of time.

An important way to understand time is in what I call 'reversed' or 'retrograde' time. Reversing time means to see time as coming in from the future. There is time that apparently comes from the past into the present, and then there is time that comes from the future, which is already complete. The future is coming into the present; it is coming into being. If we see time in this way, we can accept the perfection coming in and through us. Our job is to be open to it and to be as clear as possible inside. We can consider the completion first and then look at how we may bring it into being. The first step is to make an intention and then visualise its completion by reversing time and seeing how the completion moves towards you.

The laws of time can be found in the knowledge and practice of what is called 'the octave'. Very few people know about the octave and fewer still apply it. The way to learn about it is to experiment with it. There are a number of different natural cycles going on all the time. Likewise, there are many different octaves going on all the time. These may be octaves within an hour, a day, a week, a year or a lifetime. Whenever we agree to begin and complete something within a set amount of time we create an octave, and thus there may well be many going on at once. We can be aware of these and then, in agreement, work with them.

The notes in the octave follow the same pattern as in the standard musical octave, that is, *do, re, mi, fa, sol, la, ti, do*. Each of the notes represent certain stages of time and also qualities of energy. The more we are aware of these notes and awake to the octave itself, the more we can recognise those places where our intention is liable to be diverted and where we will need to make extra effort in order to complete what we said that we would do.

The first note of the octave has to do with intention. We start off with the note *do*, which contains all possibility and is the decision or intention. It is here we decide to complete our task by a certain time. The rest of the octave will unfold within the time that we have agreed to. We can also remember the triad of freedom, our commitment, willingness and agreement and then return to it at any time we are having difficulties in following through with our original intention. We need to persevere with our intention in order to complete the octave. The negative potential of the note *do* is apathy, in which we cannot even make a decision, let alone complete one.

Once we have made our decision we need to develop a rhythm in our action, which takes place in the note *re*. Here we can begin to take action and move towards our goal. The negative potential of the note *re* has to do with grief.

The next note is the note *mi* which is the self-consciousness of working in the octave. The negative potential of *mi* is fear, but in the note *mi* is also the potential of courage. The problem often arises here that we get caught in this sense of 'me'. We have to realise at this point that we must go on, as though we were in battle. It is a battle within not to become deviated from our original intention or stuck in fear. Here we need to have the courage to go on. The key here is gratefulness. Can we be grateful for all that has led us up to this point? We cannot go on if we are stuck in apathy, grief or fear, which are the negative potentials of the first three notes or centres in man.

The point of deviation most often occurs at the *mi-fa* interval of an octave. We are heading in a certain direction and all of a sudden we find ourselves going somewhere else. We fall asleep at this interval and some other influence comes in to sweep us away. We need to be awake and restate our intention at this point. Otherwise we are bound to get swept away by forces beyond our control, by attractions or by what we call fate. Somewhere between the *mi* and the *fa* there will probably be a distraction. This distraction may come from the outside, or it may come from our own fear of going on. Often we get deviated by attraction and the line of our intention goes off in that direction. We have to start all over again. This is known in the East as the knot of samsara, when we go around and around but never reach our goal.

We need to be aware of the *mi-fa* interval and aware of the pressure that is apt to mount here. We might have the tendency to go to sleep, get bored or go into despair at the work to be done. At this point it is helpful to have a conscious shock applied from outside ourselves to wake us up at this crucial point and remind us of our original intention. It doesn't have to be a nasty shock. It can be a butterfly landing on our hand, or a friend giving us encouragement. The time that is important is the time when it is most difficult to remember.

Although the *mi-fa* interval is difficult, it also presents us with an opportunity to do special work. If we can work on ourselves and put extra effort into this time, then we can proceed through this difficult crossing. Through gratefulness and the courage to go on, we can come into the note *fa*, which is the throne of the heart.

When we come into the note *fa*, there is a period of relaxation. This does not mean that we forget our original intention, but here we find ourselves in a place of balance between us 'doing' the work and the work 'working through' us. We are in the middle of the octave and from here the completion moves towards us with increasing speed. Time accelerates as the future comes closer and closer. The last three notes of the octave cannot really be explained in words but as we become aware of how the octave manifests within a given time frame we may notice the difference in the quality of the notes.

Finally we reach the step between *ti* and *do* which is another critical interval, the crossing into a new octave. Again the secret of moving through this interval is gratefulness, the gratefulness of having completed what we set out to do, and the willingness to let it go so that we can go on to the next step in our journey. In the completion of our original intention, working with the knowledge of the octave and other laws that govern the manifestion of life on earth, we have been able to use time consciously.

'Time is the eternal attribute of God.'

'Keep your intention before you at every step you take; you wish for freedom and you must never forget it.'

'Make the mind your friend and time will be on your side at last.'

11

Will

True will is a reflection of God's will.

Without will we cannot fulfil the will of God. God's will cannot fulfil itself without us. We need the will to do it and we need to be willing to do it. There is no use in surrendering our will to God if we do not already have will. If we do have will, we can surrender it to God and allow ourselves to be an instrument for God. Expanding on Mevlana's saying, 'I am the flute, but the music is Thine', there would be no use in giving a half-made instrument to a musician and asking him or her to play it. First we need to have something to offer and then perhaps we can be used by the higher will. Develop your will and your strengths, so that one day you may be allowed to be of service and manifest God's will here on earth.

The word 'will' is often misunderstood. Some say that we need more will and others say that we have too much. Some are proud that they have so much will and can accomplish so many things, but this 'will' may be nothing more than a desire to acquire more for themselves. Then there are those who say, 'Let Thy will be done, not mine,' without accepting their own responsibility. One person thinks he has will, but has none, and the other is afraid of having any will at all. True will is a reflection of God's will and is necessary in this world.

In order to have will we need to be completely conscious and responsible to the world around us. Will implies responsibility, and this makes real action possible. Responsibility is the ability to respond, to respond to need. In order to know what is necessary, we must be completely in our bodies and in the present moment. If we can develop this will, we have the possibility of fulfilling the will of God on earth. But it requires real work to do this. First we need the intention to develop will and to complete the tasks we set ourselves to do. We can make the intention to serve God unconditionally and thus come to love Him so much that our every expression may be the perfect expression of the highest will.

The object of will is to bring order into manifestation. For something new to be born there needs to be will and decision, because without these, our forces of habit can dictate the action. This is why G.I. Gurdjieff said that man, in his present state, cannot do anything. For the 'I' to do something implies that the 'I' exists as something conscious, having will. But often people assume that they are doing something when, in fact, they are only manifesting an unredeemed thought-form or habit. We need to be conscious and use will, which means making a conscious decision and carrying it out. We need to be able to say 'I' consciously, then 'I will'. The object of will is order, and when we are awake to order and can say 'I will' to this, then we are certainly on the way to manifesting God's will.

There are two kinds of motives for developing will. One is the love of service and the desire to help build a better world. The other is the frightening realization that we have no will and can do nothing without it. With this second realization we have to be careful not to go into self-pity and give up because we feel we cannot do anything. Many people have this sense of despair when they are not able to do what they set out to do. What we have to remember is that however many times we fail to reach our goals and fulfil our intentions, it is the perseverance, the commitment and the extra efforts we make that help develop the will and strengthen us to do better the next time. Once we can realise how little will we have, and can see how important it is, then we can make a decision to develop will.

There are various ways to develop will. One basic method is to put forth extra effort into whatever we do.

I always say that we can give ten percent more effort than we think we can. There is always at least ten percent more energy available, however tired we are. If we put in the extra efort, even if we think we can't, then we are developing will. We can make the intention to clean the house, for example, or read a book, and if it gets difficult, or we start running out of time, then we can put in ten percent more effort. When we do this we will find that we have more energy at the end than we ever thought we would have, and we will also be developing will.

Another method which is fundamental in the developing of will is to learn to make decisions and to keep our intention before us at every step of the way. The key is simply to make a decision and consciously carry it through. As we do this every day, we will be developing will. We can choose to do almost anything as long as we make the decision beforehand and then carry it out in the time and in the manner that we decided. It may not be possible to do it in the way that we originally planned. There may need to be changes, but we must at least remember our intention and attempt to do whatever is best. What is important is that we make conscious decisions and then complete them. If we do not, we will surely be tossed and turned by the hands of fate in this chaotic world. Decisions give us power to overcome the forces of hazard, and by making a decision we are given help from higher worlds.

If we do not make conscious decisions we can be controlled by the hands of fate, or by unredeemed thought-forms and desires. This is what happens when we live passively and float through life without making any decisions. If we do not take control over our lives, something else will which is not God's will. God's will comes through our will. Every decision produces some degree of creative tension, and it is within that creative tension, between our decision and the work to be done, that God's grace may enter. We need lots of perseverance and lots of patience. Perseverance is needed because we have to be able to carry on until the vision is complete, and this may take more time and energy than originally planned.

Patience is needed because the vision cannot be completed until the time is right. Patience is the distance between vision and manifestation.

Many times I've heard people say, 'I know I made that decision but I can't do it now because something else has come up and I don't feel like it any more.' We are often tyrannised by our feelings, and think these temporary feelings are so important that we forget what needs to be done. Don't allow yourselves to be used by your emotions. Just get out of bed and get on with it. What comes up will go out in the same way if you just let it be and do something useful. Stop worrying about yourselves, stop complaining; see what needs to be done and do it. Otherwise the tyranny can continue for years, never changing until we say, 'I will'. The more we develop will the less we are lost in our own problems and tossed by the hands of fate.

All of us, at some time or another, experience fear. This fear can be very useful; we may be in danger of some kind and need to run quickly. But many times fear is unnecessary or it arises from our fear of a new challenge in life. Whatever it is, fear can be conquered by a decision. It doesn't help to fight fear because it will fight back, and it doesn't help to be embarrassed about fear or to think of ourselves as cowards, because fear is something that we all have to some degree or another. We can conquer fear by making a decision. In other words, as we start to take action with total commitment, the fear will slowly dissolve. See what can be done, make a decision to do it, then begin to act on that decision. The fear may still be there, which may be a healthy carefulness, but it won't control us any more.

When we are identified with our bodies, our emotions or our thoughts, we are caught in their tyranny. Do not allow them to tyrannise you. They are not meant to control you. This would be like the donkey leading us to where it wants to go, instead of us deciding where we need to go. Working with our bodies, emotions or thoughts is like training a horse. We don't want to break the spirit of the horse because we will take something away from it. Instead we want to acknowledge the Spirit so that the spirit of the horse will recognise the spirit in us. Then there will be a bond of friendship and once there is friendship there can be cooperation. In a like manner we need to make friends with our body, our emotions and our mind. Do not let these things rule over you. Learn not to identify with your reactions and your thoughts. It is just not useful and, if you do, you will never go beyond your habitual patterns of conditioning. The same patterns will merely continue in different ways, not only for us, but into the next generation as well.

What we identify with is not necessarily even our thoughts, but merely thought-forms floating about with a desire to manifest somewhere. When we identify with these unredeemed thought-forms we are being taken further and further from the real truth of our being. Ninety-five percent of all mental illness in the world is due to the tyranny of the elemental kingdom over us, and the way this manifests is through the body, emotions and thoughts. This world was made for man and woman, not the other way around. All is contained within the human being, all the elements and all the kingdoms. Even the angelic kingdom is 'within', and is dependent upon us, because the angels do not have bodies. The world is here for us, but unless we are conscious and in control of the many forces, we will only be tyrannised by those forces.

You are not your body. It has brought you to where you are now, but you are not the body. You are not your emotions. Your emotions may be very important to you. Do not deny them, as the psychologists say, but understand that you are not an emotion. You are not your thoughts. Thoughts can be very useful (if you hadn't thought about some of this you might not continue to be interested), but you are not your thoughts.

If we are not the body, emotions or thoughts, who are we? Through will we can gather ourselves together into one dynamic point from which we can serve life. If we are not in control of our body, our emotions and our mind, then we are scattered across the universe. We are asked to surrender ourselves to God—not just a portion of our self, but all of our self. Unless we are in control of our energies and have all of our self together at one point in time, which is this moment, we have nothing to give to God. If we are to give of ourselves we need to be fully present and together. Give of yourselves totally and completely, because there is no other way.

If we develop a one-pointed aim, then we bring everything into this one point. If we can have one great aim in life, we can direct all of our self to this. This is how we can develop will. The whole of our being can come together in one great aim. And through this coming together will is developed and conscience awakened. True conscience is a direct perception of the divine will. It is true knowledge from awakened intelligence. From this awakened intelligence, or conscience, we are able to be compassionate towards all things in life. We can see everything from a greater perspective, not in comparison, or in terms of good and evil, but seeing things just as they are, while realising our own responsibility in participating in the divine will.

Only through the development of will can the intelligence be awakened. Intelligence is a divine quality which is already inherent within us and needs to be awakened through will. It is said that you cannot teach an unintelligent person. This is true because unless the intelligence is awakened there can be no recognition of the truth. It is through the quality of intelligence that we understand the truth and the divine plan. One of the keys in awakening intelligence is to observe oneself. We need knowledge and the greatest knowledge is the knowledge of ourselves. It is by observing ourselves that we can come to know ourselves. Begin to know yourself and the intelligence will start to awaken from within. Then you have something to offer God and the Work.

12

Transformation

The time is not tomorrow. It is now.

The work of transformation is dependent upon practices. We might be given all the best theories in the world but these will not necessarily do anything unless they are put into practice. When it comes to practices each human being is different and unique. One pair of shoes does not fit everyone. The same practice may produce different results in different people. This is why a living teacher and a living school is so helpful, because it is very difficult, if not impossible, for the conditioned mind to lead itself out of its own trappings; and it is very difficult, if not dangerous, to assume that the same things will benefit all people. There are some practices and ideas, however, that are more universal, which can be useful to anyone.

The purpose of all practice is transformation. This is what a 'real' school is about. Most people come to a spiritual school to get something for themselves. They think that the practices are for their self-development when, in fact, they are for the transformation of the self, not its development. Transformation involves sacrificing our concepts of the self; otherwise there is no transformation. It involves real change, and for something new to come about, something else has to die away.

Another misconception is that we can transform ourselves by ourselves. Transformation happens to us and for us, depending on the degree of work we do. People often talk about working on themselves without knowing what this means. You cannot transform personality with personality. When you work on yourself what is working on what? If you try to destroy the ego with the ego, you create a thousand-headed serpent. So what can you do? It is said that love can turn even copper into gold. Love will melt the personality, because love redeems all into itself. We have to allow ourselves to be loved, which is to be transformed in the fire of love.

We keep thinking we are so very important. We keep thinking and talking about 'me': 'Me, me, me.' If we cannot get past this sense of 'me', we cannot take the next step in the octave, which is a step into the heart, a step into love. We are not important, at least we are not more important than this great, wonderful universe. We are no more important than anyone else, but we think we are with all the demands we make every day. We demand others to be as we want, we demand our own happiness, we demand our important experiences. As long as we demand anything for ourselves we are stuck in the 'me' centre, and we can never cross 'the great water'.

The secret to crossing the great water is in the breaking of what I call the dome, which is between the solar plexus and the heart. The dome acts as a filter between the higher and lower aspects of ourselves. It is actually a spiritual protection, so that we do not open too quickly and be overwhelmed by the light of the higher powers. When we are ready to go beyond our spiritual virginity, it is possible to gradually relax the dome and move our centre of gravity from the solar plexus to the heart. The resistance needs to melt. It is an opening of the heart, which can only come about when we have gained freedom from the dominance of our lower nature, and from this, dormant faculties and intelligences will begin to awaken. The habitual patterns start to dissolve and new impulses from a higher order begin to move us.

As we move our centre of gravity into the heart, a higher energy is released which can then awaken dormant faculties beyond the senses we usually know. The key to relaxing the dome and entering the heart is to do with breath and the attitude of service. If we can learn to breathe out love from the heart in service to all around us, then we are certainly helping in God's work, which cannot happen without us.

We are given this opportunity as human beings to participate in the divine plan. Then, in the arms of God's compassion, we return to our true nature to be one with the Beloved and thus fulfil God's will on earth. We are the bridge between heaven and earth, and we can return to God through the sacrifice of all that we think we are, while at the same time acting as a channel for that divine will to manifest on earth. In this way we are turning to God and to the earth like a vortex, or spiral, moving up and down at the same time. We turn to God so that the will of God may manifest through us.

This is the way of service, but before we can hope to be of service, we need to have knowledge of certain basic laws and gain control over certain aspects of ourselves. We cannot do this on our own without some help from others who have already walked the Path. We need to be receptive to the knowledge that others are willing to give, and we need to allow ourselves to be transformed. Unless the time is right, nothing can be done. We can be taught the greatest secrets of the universe but it will make no difference at all if the time is not right. The time becomes right when there is receptivity. The Work is very much alive, but it needs receptivity to manifest itself.

Sometimes in this Work we come across forces within us and in the world that do not want to allow the Work to happen. These forces do all that they can to stop the flow of spiritual grace into the world. They try to stop the Work, because they do not want change. They actually struggle against the Work, and so we have to struggle with ourselves to remain awake. Once we are involved with the Work there is a tremendous flow of energy. We are dealing with enormous energies. Energy follows thought and so if we are not completely pure or united with the One, which is inevitable, because we live in this relative world with all of its relative problems, there is bound to be some 'thought' in us that can lead us astray and impede the Work.

If we let ourselves be led astray, if we let ourselves fall asleep for too long, disorder will soon take over. This is evident when it comes to running a centre for healing or transformation. If we let it go, if we let our intention to serve drop just a little, the forces of disorder soon set in, and the result is a drain in energy and a growing confusion. I've seen it happen so many times. We have to keep the space for the Work spotlessly clean and in complete order, and we have to watch these things very carefully.

We are given space and time, and it is our responsibility as human beings to make correct use of them. In this space there is possibility. What we do with our space is up to us. If we don't do something with it, we are wasting time. Let us make space for beauty to enter. Let beauty come on earth 'as it is in heaven'. Each moment of beauty that fills our space is indeed creating heaven on earth. Every moment can be magical if we realise that it is the only time there is. *Space without time would be a void with no possibility.* Time without space would be a pointless waste of energy.

What do we fill our space with? What kind of thought? What attractions? Are we preparing a space for divine possibility to enter? Remember that energy follows thought and thought attracts its own kind. This means that we, as human beings on this planet, have a great responsibility in the way we use thought. Every thought has a sound and every sound carries a weight of meaning within it. Thought comes in many different colours and vibrations. All thought wishes to express itself through the world of feeling and into the world of form. We are approximately eighty percent water, and water is a conductor of electricity. A thought-form is an electrical impulse. Therefore, we are full of a lot of thought, most of which is probably useless. If we breathe consciously, that water can flow continuously, and then we will not be full of so much stagnant thought.

It is hard not to let thought rule us because the food of the mind is thought and comparison. Every negative thought or judgement holds us in a prison of our own creation. It can also affect everyone else in the world, because everything is interconnected. We need to 'eat' these thoughts, transforming them into pure thought, which is the food for our spiritual growth. If we can sacrifice them, or allow them to be transformed into light, we are feeding our inner being and freeing ourselves from the tyranny of thought. When we live in freedom we can free others. If we can live for the freedom of others we become free ourselves; we can become willing servants of God, dedicated to service in the love of God and all beings on this planet.

As we serve others so we serve God. This is a completely new orientation to life, and out of this comes a real change in our being. Our ability to serve is dependent upon our commitment, willingness and agreement, the triad of freedom. Through this triad we are freed from the cocoon of our conditioned self; we are liberated from the tyranny of thought and self-centred feelings. Through our commitment, willingness and agreement we are able to fulfil the true destiny of the soul. This is the sacrifice of oneself in transformation, and it can only happen from the heart. The heart is the altar of sacrifice. As we move into the heart and give everything up in love, our whole being is burned in the fire of love, as in Mevlana's wish for 'Burning, only burning'.

13

Service

Our duty, our responsibility, is to serve the Work of God.
This is our obligation in being conscious human beings.

What is the purpose of life? Now, that is a good question. Seldom do we question the purpose of life and what we are doing here. We think we are awake when we are asleep. We are tossed about by the waves of fate, and eventually we come to the point where we never again question the purpose of life. We may even think we are doing something new, but probably we are merely repeating the past in another disguise. We think we have our own thoughts, but in reality there are myriads of thought-forms floating around the world looking for someone to manifest through.

To be 'awake' means to be awake to our higher possibilities. We have the choice to live life asleep and be at the mercy of a fate determined by outer circumstances, or to live life awake to destiny, responding to the higher calling of a divine purpose. This certainly requires work, work on ourselves, in order to go beyond our limited, narrow minds and our continually reacting emotions.

In many cases our lives have been governed by patterns from the past that stand in the way of our potential to serve. It is possible to leave the past behind and search for a new pattern in our lives. The pattern of this new possibility is in life itself; in fact, it *is* life itself. Life manifests the perfect pattern, and when we come to know this and live in harmony with it, then we come into the stream of service.

One of the difficulties in coming upon the way of service is that we are so cluttered with preconceived notions as to what 'the spiritual path' is about. Therefore we need to work on ourselves to break down this conditioning, so that we can be of service to that which is 'outside of time' needing to be 'in time'. No one can make that commitment for us. It has to come from our own heart and willingness. We have to take that plunge ourselves, surrendering totally to the path that leads to complete unity. It takes courage, honesty and a passionate yearning to know the truth.

We really do have a purpose, but the difficulty is that we approach this purpose with the same conditioned mind that keeps us from fulfilling it. Our search is often conditioned by the ego's desire to grow and expand itself. In fact, the false 'I' will do anything to protect itself from its assimilation into the real. The ego will be attracted to those teachers and ideas that feed its own illusion of self-importance, and it will run from those teachers who challenge its own self-righteousness. This is why we need an intention that is beyond time and even beyond self. If we can find and hold to an intention that is beyond time, beyond the conditioned mind, then we can possibly allow ourselves to be assimilated into the real. The real work of transformation has nothing to do with the placation of our self-righteousness. It involves an assimilation into the stream of service, which brings us in touch with the real world, and to come into the stream of service we need to set our intention outside of time.

Usually our intentions have to do with comparison. We want one thing because we don't want the other. We move south because we don't like the cold, or we move north because we don't like the heat. Our intentions move us from one thing to another, but it never seems to be just right. This is because we are in comparison and have not accepted the unity and perfection of life. If our intention is towards unity, not duality, then we cannot make such comparisons. An intention coming out of comparison can only recreate the duality of the conditioned mind. We need to set our intention outside of time, within and for unity. The moment we do this we are led by the divine will towards where we need to be and in that way we can put our talents to the best possible use.

We might have entered the spiritual path without really knowing why, without understanding our motives and intentions, but if we are lucky we will come to the realization that we are here to serve life. We are here to serve humanity and the planet as a whole, which has to do with everyday life. It has to do with everyday people and everyday things. We serve what is nearest to us. In order to serve we need to know what service is. We need knowledge, for love is not enough. Love is all around but we still need knowledge to manifest it. The extent of the goodness that comes from the willing heart is dependent upon the degree of realization and knowledge of the heart. We are here to be conscious, God-conscious, which means being conscious within the knowledge of the unity of God.

Knowing our purpose in life can only come about as we begin to put every part of ourselves into the way of service. Serve *in* the light. When you have understood and accepted God's light, then I can say to you, 'Let your light shine,' because it will be God's light that shines. Be so empty that there is only the light of God shining out for everyone. But unless you are empty, you may just be shining your own big 'ego' all over the place. Still, you have to go on. You have to continue working on yourself, without really knowing where you are on the Path, and you have to continue to serve the moment in whatever way you can. Don't be afraid to get out and serve life. Nobody is perfect. You don't have to be a perfect saint to serve and help the Work unfold. You have to begin somewhere and that is wherever you are now. Maybe you feel incapable of really doing anything, but still, you have to work on something, because no one else is going to do the work for you. God can't do it all, so don't leave it all up to God. Even if your ego gets in the way, even if you are not so pure yet, even if you are just beginning on this path, never deny the possibility that there is something you can do. You might fall back or get a little lost at times, but you have to go on.

I encourage you to go on. You can, you have to do it, because there is no one else to do it for you. I can't do it for you. I can't be you. I can't live your life, and nobody else can. God is not going to do it for you from some great 'heaven' in the sky or wherever, because God is not separate from you or this world. God has no eyes but yours, nor ears but yours, no hands but yours. You will have to be the one who does the Work. You will have to manifest the truth. You will have to stand in His name, which is in the perfection of love, harmony and beauty.

The Sufis say that God gives us everything and there are two things we must give back, which are servility and obedience. God can't give us those two things. God does not force those qualities upon us. It is for us to give willingly, in love. Service is knowing the meaning of the purpose of life on earth and thus serving the work of God. Our duty, our responsibility is to serve the work of God. This is our obligation in being conscious human beings on the planet. Most people cannot do this yet. Most do not even know it is possible, and many do not want to do it anyway. Still, it is our obligation, even if we fail most of the time. We can look back in history and see many mistakes, but we can be grateful for these mistakes, because through mistakes we learn. The greatest mistake of all is leaving it all up to God, because God needs us. We must do the necessary work, and to deny our role, to deny our obligation, is to deny God in each one of us.

Either we concern ourselves only with our own salvation, or we consider ourselves as integral parts of the whole, having a responsibility to the overall purpose. Each person has an equal responsibility in the potential functioning of the planet. We share in this overall picture, and the understanding of this can bring about a sense of true brotherhood. If only we could be totally responsible to this moment in everything we do, in every breath we take, in every thought we have, then this would have a remarkable effect on every one of God's creatures. If we are responsible to all the kingdoms, all the lives on this planet, then we are in the Work. To come upon the Work is easy, but to become completely involved means a sacrifice of our lives to the whole of creation.

A good friend of mine once helped me through a time of personal difficulty. He took me out into the garden, and as we walked around he kept pointing out various rocks, flowers and trees that were there for me to see. He continued doing this to help me get more and more grounded and into the present moment. Then, when I was finally grounded enough, he said, 'Reshad, you need to make a sacrifice,' and he walked off, leaving me alone to ponder the meaning of this. He knew that I knew what I needed to do, but I needed to hear it from someone I trusted. I made that sacrifice and was able to go on, but before this I could not do what I needed to do, because I would not give something up. There is often something that holds us back, and that is what we will not give up. Whether it be a habit, a belief, a resentment or a situation, there is something blocking the way from going on to the next step. That is why sacrifice is always needed along the Way.

When we first enter a real school or a path of transformation we are carried along with enough enthusiasm to provide the impetus to work on whatever is given, whether we understand it or not, and whether we like it or not. Everything is new and we are willing to try anything. We will gladly scrub a floor with a toothbrush or do whatever exercises, however difficult. The Way may not be easy, life may not be so easy, but we proceed, challenging test after test, fulfilling whatever we are asked to do. We put ourselves second to the task. We surrender our own immediate desires to what is needed in the moment. We are asked to give up our selfishness to the work at hand. The word 'need' is stressed and what we want becomes second to this.

When we were little children we were taught what is needed. We may have wanted all the sweets we could eat, but we were taught what the body actually needed, and we had to sacrifice what we wanted for what we needed. The parent has to teach the child what is good and needed. Then, the child begins to learn what is needed, but there is often a struggle along the way, for both the parent and the child.

On the path of transformation we might very willingly begin to sacrifice our wants, due to our initial enthusiasm, but eventually our wants rise up to struggle against this.

There may come a time when we really question what this 'Path' is all about. We might ask ourselves, 'Do I really want to do this? Am I willing to complete this?' These questions are good, because we would be foolish to continue doing something without ever questioning the meaning of it for our own lives and the good of others. In our questioning, and the decisions that come out of this, our wants may start to become united with our needs. Through the questioning we see more of the purpose of the Path and we begin to really want to do what is needed. We want to complete what we need to do, because we see that it is useful to ourselves and the world. Finally, there is the possibility that our wish becomes one with God's desire. 'God's want' becomes 'our need'. The need of the moment and our wanting to fulfil the need become a spontaneous act of service.

If we can accept the challenges of life willingly, then we can proceed through whatever difficulties stand in our way. We will see the need and we will want, with all our heart, to fulfil the task. We will see the reason, the purpose behind the task and, if the going gets rough we will not get lost in resentment about doing it in the first place. Through all of this we need patience and perseverance. Without patience and perseverance it is all too easy to slip back from the original enthusiasm. We might then feel resentment or apathy toward the task, or complain how the world is treating us poorly, and we might even give up the work altogether, which would be a waste of an opportunity to serve God's will and fulfil our own destiny.

Can we be honest with ourselves? Do we have the original enthusiasm to carrying us through? Are we questioning the work we are doing? If we are questioning, then we need to reconsider the original aim. The original aim, however naïve at first, was perhaps an impulse of divine love that brought us to this point where we are now. We now need to reconsider what we really want. Do we want to serve God's will, which is dependent upon our desire to serve? We can serve God's will when we recognise our own completion in God. Then there is no difference between our desire and God's. Whatever is needed we will want to do it. God needs us. The Work needs us, and the world needs us. In reality, there is only One Being. There is only One Truth. We serve only One. We cannot serve two masters at the same time, so we have to make a choice. Either we continue sleep-walking through life, only thinking about ourselves, and repeating the patterns of our uncontrollable wants, or we sacrifice and commit ourselves totally to serving the greater purpose of life.

To enter the path of service deliberately is to enter the stream of conscious evolution. There are two kinds of evolution. One is organic and the other is conscious. Organic evolution continues onwards without conscious intention. It is the slow and unconscious force of evolution, of which all life is a part. There is an ongoing evolution from the mineral kingdom through the vegetable kingdom to the animal kingdom and on through man, and we can understand this scientifically, as well as mystically. At the same time, though, there is a possibility for conscious evolution, which is only possible through a human being. Both streams of evolution are necessary, but conscious evolution cannot take place without our conscious efforts.

Conscious evolution can only come about if we are conscious. Thus, it is our obligation in life to wake up to whatever is happening and whatever is needed. Conscious evolution is determined by our degree of awareness. It requires awareness and intention. The implications of our being awake right now at this very moment are far-reaching, beyond what we can possibly understand. Evolution is taking place right now through us, depending upon our degree of awareness. Whatever we are doing, whether it be washing our hands, eating food, breathing the air or making love, we have the possibility to participate in conscious evolution. But first we have to be conscious, and then we can begin to make conscious efforts. This is what serves conscious evolution, and we begin by waking up to the need of the moment. Nothing can happen unless we are awake in the present moment.

Service comes about first with awareness and respect. If you are not awake, you will never know what to do, and if you cannot respect the needs of others, you won't bother to be awake. You cannot know what to do unless you are awake to the need. Without being awake you will probably be attending to one particular task while a much more important one goes unattended. Unless you are awake to need you won't know what to do. First, we need to be awake to where we are now and what we need. Then we can be awake to what another person may need, then to what a group may need, then a city and then the planet. But first we have to take care of what is in front of us. This is our responsibility. It is our duty to find out what we can do and what needs to be done. This is our obligation in being born man and woman: to discover what we can do to serve the life we have been given.

To be of service we need knowledge. Love is not enough, *because we have to know how to apply love,* and for this we need knowledge. Knowledge it not acquired; it is given when we are ready to receive it, when we are awake in the present moment to receive it. Knowledge and service go hand in hand, and what is helpful one moment might not be helpful in the next. Nobody can really tell us exactly what is needed in all circumstances, because no two moments are the same, just as no two people are the same. The way of service is to be awake in the present moment, then we can spontaneously act from love and knowledge.

Service is spontaneously acting in the moment for the good of the whole. But it does not just happen by itself. You have to do it, and in order to do it you need will. You need to have will in order to surrender willingly to love, then real action can take place in the moment. Real action has to be right in the moment, right in the moment of need. It can't wait. It has to be an immediate response, and that is what I mean by spontaneous. It is conscious and spontaneous at the same time. The action itself is a response to love. You are so in love that there is no hesitation, no thinking about it. You just do or say what is needed at that moment, as a conscious, spontaneous response for the good of the whole. Don't wait and don't think. So many times people miss the chance to help somebody because they have to think about it first. You will always be late if you have to think about it. Just do it, don't be afraid. Trust that you can help and do it. If a child is about to run in front of a bus, don't wait to see what happens. When it's time to act it's time to move. Don't wait, because the opportunity will disappear faster than you can think.

Sometimes you can be of service when it appears to be otherwise. There are even times when you are so humble or the time is so right, that you are able to be of service despite yourself. Sometimes you can be of service when you appear to be making a mistake. Don't be ashamed of your weaknesses, your problems or your uncertainties. Love all of yourself, including your weaknesses. In this way we can have compassion for other people's weaknesses. Weaknesses are not necessarily bad, though we usually judge ourselves and others by these weaknesses. Instead of condemning the weaknesses, try loving them. Maybe all they need is a bit of love to grow into strengths. If you have a loving heart and have dedicated yourself to the path of service, you can be of service despite your weaknesses. You may even be of service by presenting your weaknesses so that someone else can love and help you. Who is helping who? There is only God, and none of this is outside God. Thank God for our weaknesses and pain so that we can serve each other in the One Family of God. It is not that we want the pain or problems to remain as such, but we can love them without hatred or denial. In that love, which is the love of God, they can be transformed into strength and joy.

It is as much our duty to love ourselves and give ourselves what we need, as it is to serve others. It is our duty to balance our lives in a way that is loving to ourselves, our families, our friends, our communities and our world. There are exceptional people who give their lives to serving others and the world, without thought for themselves. Yet, we need to take care of ourselves too. It is important to give to yourself as well as others. Some people give and give and give, but forget their own well-being. We have to give to ourselves as well. How many people really love themselves? The paradox of this is that you cannot really love yourself until you are empty of yourself. When you are empty you can really love. Then love is able to manifest through you. So allow yourself to be loved, and do not neglect to take care of yourself.

Do not be shy about loving yourself. I'll give you a tip about loving yourself. Start with the body. Take some time to really look at yourself. See the beauty of your body. See yourself as a unique manifestation of the beauty of God. In Sufism we say that the sole purpose of love is beauty. Your beauty is God's purpose. Don't get frightened or ashamed about this—because initially it may be difficult to see yourself this way—but begin to see the beauty in yourself and agree to it. And know the beauty in all aspects of yourself, from your body to your feelings to your mind. Know your beauty, and then you will be able to radiate that beauty, and thus others will know God's beauty through you.

We are given this life. It is a gift. Therefore, we might consider what we can give in return. One thing that we can give is our gratefulness for being alive, our gratefulness for having this body, these feelings, this mind, this world. We are given so much. We are also given a way, a way to serve life. God provides us with this. If we are awake we can learn what we are given to learn, and see what is given for us to do. God provides what we need. God provides a way for us to grow and serve life, and it is up to us to understand this and use whatever comes our way. We can use what we are given in life in order to serve life.

It is like the breath, in that we can breathe in what we need and breathe out a distillation of this for the good of the world. The key here is gratefulness because through gratefulness we can fully receive all that is given to us. In gratefulness we can give back our love to the world. Mevlana said, 'Gratefulness is the key to will'. It is also the key to service. The best attitude we can have in giving is being grateful for the opportunity to give. We are here to give, to give all of ourselves in total commitment to life. This is what we are asked to do in reciprocation for the gift of life given to us.

One of the main practices I have given to people over the years is the prayer, 'May I be allowed to be of service'. When you are given an opportunity to serve you can be grateful for such a privilege. Service is a great opportunity. Take advantage of it, because we are not always given such opportunities. To be given an opportunity implies a certain degree of trust.

When we say that a person is trustworthy it means that they can be trusted to do what they say they are going to do. When we see that a person fulfils what is asked of them or what they promise to do, then they become worthy of our trust. And if they do even more, they show us a certain integrity that cannot be forgotten. It is difficult to trust people who don't fulfil what they have agreed to do. Often we have difficulty entrusting children with responsibilities, or trusting that they can take care of things properly, but we can teach children about trust and trustworthiness by being trustworthy ourselves. We may even have difficulty in trusting God, especially if we think of God as something distant from us and this world. But let us remember that God is here with us and not separate from us.

It takes trust to remain grateful for whatever is given, in the knowledge that this will surely lead us on the path of service. The Way is coming towards us all the time, and the knowledge of this leads to trust. It leads to patience, for we will have to be patient. Things do not necessarily fall into place easily. The Path does not always go in the direction we want it to, or expect it to. We need to be patient and trusting that things are working out in ways that are hard for us to understand.

We are given a way, but it is up to us whether we follow it or not. We are given so much in this life, and if we are really grateful for all that we are given, then we will spontaneously want to give back whatever we can. It does not just happen on its own. We need will and we need to be willing, because if we are not, we will resent what is given for us to do. Once we are allowed an opportunity to serve, it is up to us to bring it forth. This requires will. It also requires love and knowledge, which in essence is God's love and knowledge. Our work is to be purified vehicles for the love and knowledge of God.

14

Cooperation

Let us all share our knowledge with each other and work hand in hand to bring forth the world to come.

As human beings we are responsible for this planet. This planet is given to us. The Sufis say that the universe was made for man. There is a responsibility in this, and within each of us is the inherent knowledge necessary to put this responsibility to good use. We must re-establish the balance between ourselves and the other kingdoms of nature. We can make good use of this planet and serve the divine order inherent within it. All possibility exists here for us, if we give agreement to it, recognise it and serve it. In a sense, there is nothing but possibility, and yet it will remain only a possibility unless we work together to fulfil the destiny of human existence. This planet is the expression of divine love. It is a womb of divine love, and we can bring forth a world radiating love and perfection, if only we give agreement to it. This is the extraordinary miracle that God has granted us.

We are the custodians of this planet. Who else can do it? The animals can do what they have instinctively learned to do, but they cannot look after the planet. Animals and plants fulfil their respective functions unconsciously. As human beings we need consciously to understand the world we live in and who we are, in order to fulfil that purpose for which we are here. We need to come to an awareness of natural law, which is divine law, and participate in something that can only fulfil itself through our conscious agreement. Without conscious man, who knows himself and his place in the universe, the divine law cannot manifest upon earth and fulfilment of divine perfection cannot come into being. God needs man, and it is man who stands between heaven and earth.

Great changes are necessary at this time in history, and we, in some way, must be part of this process of change. This is why many people find themselves in transition, because they are trying to find a new path for themselves. We find ourselves between an old order and a new one that has yet to unfold. The sense of urgency is obvious to anyone who is able to wake up to the situation as it really is. Not everyone has the courage to do this and see what may force them to make the necessary changes in their lives. However there will be an eventual awakening, and the danger in this is that it could produce such a shock that panic may ensue and the structure we so much depend upon for survival may collapse too fast. Are we prepared for such difficulties and problems? Inevitably, there needs to be cooperation between all those people who do see the crisis at hand and who have at least a glimpse of the way through it.

The old order of civilization is over and we are now ready to take one of the greatest steps in the evolution of the planet. Probably at no other time in history has there been such a need for cooperation between all groups of people, between all societies and nations. Finally, we are faced with our responsibility for taking care of this planet. We must end the neglect and greed that has had such a devastating effect. Through greed and ignorance, man has raped the planet and created chaos upon the earth. We are at the edge of destroying this beautiful experiment of life on earth, when we were meant to take care of it; but let us not lay blame and create more resentment, for the cause of it all is ignorance. It is time to wake up. We need knowledge. We need understanding, and then we can surrender to the reality of what we need to do.

Unless we face up to this responsibility soon and fulfil what we need to do, it may be too late. The supports for the old order are collapsing, so we must begin now to build a new world based upon a higher order of life. A time of crisis is also a time of great possibilities. As the old order splits apart, the new order may begin. We are standing on the brink of time, on the razor's edge of evolution. Behind us is the wonderful past, which has shaped our lives and brought us here to this platform on which we stand. Ahead of us stands that which must come forth.

Evolution does not go in easy stages. There are quantum leaps within basic cycles. We are in the middle of the crossing point of two great cycles. This is the end of our civilization in corruption and the beginning of a great civilization in truth. We have a very short time left in which to work for this and our efforts may be resisted by every form of orthodoxy, which will not want to give up its power. To allow the necessary changes to take place means taking a huge step into the unknown.

This transition is not going to be easy. What is more, it won't happen unless we do something about it. Nothing can happen without our effort and without our sacrifice. Then there is a possibility of change.

We cannot even consider personality in this, neither mine nor yours, nor anybody else's. There is work to be done, a new age to be built. The work is too important merely to worry about personalities or who does this or that. We have to begin now. You and I have to build a new age, because we recognise the necessity for it. We understand that it will take work and plenty of sacrifice. Not everyone will help, because not everyone understands the immense importance of this work and this transition. Don't look for help anywhere outside yourselves. We will have help though. Help will come, but we have to begin.

A new world can be born out of this recognition. Some people are beginning to understand the laws of the spiritual path, which are not separate from life. The spiritual path is all about life. Life is precious and has much to teach; study life. We have entered a new age and there are new laws of life to be understood. There is a new order emerging, the divine order, which is perfect order. We need to be able to give up the old ways and commit ourselves to new ways of living, ways that will serve the planet and the generations to come. We can do this by recognizing the divine order.

What we are involved with is actually much greater than the mind can comprehend, but still we need to plan for the future. We need to visualise in terms of at least two hundred years and yet very few people even consider the next generation. There was a time when people planted and built for many generations to come. They visualised what would be needed and began the process of planting seeds for the future. They knew about the land, the trees and the plants. They considered how each thing would grow and affect all the others. They knew the healing properties of plants and where they would grow best according to the overall ecology. They knew the perfection of the natural world and worked consciously with it.

We need to come into an attitude of cooperation, and this applies to the invisible worlds as well as the physical. There are inner laws and invisible energies within the physical world that need to be respected, and which can be used for the benefit of mankind. We need to love the land and the earth in a very deep way. This does not mean that we allow the elements to rule over us. It means that we will some day recognise the tremendous powers and energies inherent within the earth, and learn to cooperate and make friends with these, so that all life will flourish. The knowledge of this has actually existed for a long time, but it is now ready to fulfil itself on a global scale.

There is a whole system of energies in flow around the planet, which fertilize and maintain the existence of life on earth. Because of our lack of cooperation with the kingdoms of nature, these energies have been depleted and the flow and distribution has been painfully blocked. This energy is the cohesive force of all organisms and organizations, and if it continues to be disrupted, there will inevitably be a breakdown of all order in social, political, spiritual, and even biological functions, as we witness in the breakdown of the immune system.

Available to us are sources of energy of a higher order, which can be tapped and used to heal the problems we have created. As we tap into these higher energies we must plunge boldly into the immediacy of living, without looking back or attempting to repeat what others have done before us. We must move forward in love, in the knowledge that life cannot be what it was before.

Let us live a life of service, so that the higher energies and the work of God may manifest through us and into the waiting world. Let us realise that we are One, that there is only One Absolute Being. Let us learn to respect each other's paths, knowing that it is the diversity within the One that reveals the glory and miracle of life. Let us all share our knowledge with each other and work hand in hand to bring forth the world to come, the great Work on earth. Let us be responsible for ourselves and the world around us. Let us be open to the highest source of energy, which is Love, the cause of all creation.

In the search for truth there will always be different confrontations. The first confrontation will be between those who know and those who do not want to know. The second confrontation will be between those who know and those who will have to know. We can first of all see this within ourselves, because there is so much of us that does not want to know. If we enter a path towards the truth, or even aspire towards the truth, then inevitably there will be a confrontation between those aspects of ourselves which do know and those that do not want to know. There are aspects of ourselves that do not want to know the truth, that do not want to follow the truth. These denying aspects do not want to accept their total dependence upon God, or let us say the whole. They think they are self-sufficient and self-important.

No matter what we do or how accomplished we are, there is only one way to freedom and that is in the knowledge of our dependence upon God. We can have an abundance of material possessions, computers and wonderful technologies, but if we do not accept this dependence, then we really have nothing, because none of these things will last. The only thing that can last is the everlasting Spirit, or love of God. The only real freedom is in becoming a servant of God. This sounds like a contradiction, because we think of a servant as not free, but the servant of God is free because he lives in and for the truth, and the truth is everlasting.

Those who can see the greater purpose of life, and are willing to serve it, are free in their dependence upon God. Together we can realise our interconnectedness with all life and then help build a new and beautiful world out of love and knowledge for our children and our children's children.

15

Brotherhood

A real spiritual group, or school, does not impose itself upon the individual, but provides a place of service and an opportunity for transformation.

Once we realise our dependence upon the truth and that we must learn to live by certain fundamental laws that govern our existence on this planet, then we can begin to build a new world together, a world based upon the divine order. First, we need to realise that we are all part of the family of God. In essence, we are all brothers and sisters of One Spirit, which is life itself. Throughout history those who have realised this essential truth, and have dedicated themselves to serving it, have formed groups and communities, which existed in different forms and by different names. Many were set up for a specific purpose and also functioned as schools of transformation. Now is a time when new brotherhoods and new communities are being built, but we all need to remember that we are serving the same essential purpose. There's really only One Brotherhood, One Family of God.

There are times when we are lucky enough to have an experience of real brotherhood, when we completely respect each other without any judgement and without any dogma or form. This is what real brotherhood is about. It is not restricted to any one gender but is, of course, about brothers and sisters.

Brotherhood has to include all of life, because all life is interconnected and we all need each other to fulfil our purpose here on earth. We cannot separate ourselves from the rest of life, from other people, from animals, plants or the elements. If we exclude anything or anyone, this is not the kind of brotherhood I am speaking about. Some people retreat into the forest or the mountains to get away from man, but the danger in this is that one can become lost in the elemental world and lose touch with what it means to be human.

We cannot do anything alone because we are all interconnected. This is why agreement is so necessary. When we realise the interconnectedness of all things, we might understand the meaning of the saying, 'You cannot pick a flower without the troubling of a star.' The power of God manifests through agreement. The many working groups and communities are all part and parcel of the need for agreement in the relative world. As form breaks down around us, as religions and systems break down, we will need this sense of universal brotherhood and agreement.

Brotherhood must be based upon cooperation, and cooperation can only be based upon knowledge. We all need to work together; we need to know about each other. We need to know what the other is doing so that we do not duplicate the work. For example, one community does not make baskets if another community nearby is already making them. Only so many baskets are needed, therefore one group produces baskets while the other group produces something else. This is simple cooperation.

Brotherhood involves cooperating to get done whatever is needed at any one time. We are brought together into a brotherhood through need. Even if we do not have all the knowledge necessary, it doesn't matter, because we can work as a team. We can cooperate together in one brotherhood. Often, intuitively, we are brought together for some particular task which might not be realised for many years. Whatever it is, brotherhood comes out of need, and it requires cooperation to keep it going.

We have to prove we are worthy to be friends. We have to prove our loyalty and trust-worthiness. That requires effort on our part. We can't just leave that to God. It is up to us to treat each other with love and respect. We need to make that commitment individually, and together. We need to make an effort. We need to make a sacrifice. It will not work otherwise. A brotherhood cannot be based upon egos and personalities. It cannot be based upon fears, resentments, greed or anything that separates us from the rest of the world. It cannot be used as a barricade against the world. It needs to be based upon respect for others and service in the world, not seclusion from it. This may mean some sacrifice, but all great people have sacrificed consciously for the world and the future.

We need to have agreement and cooperation, and this implies trust. The quality of trust is often difficult to realise. Our trust is usually connected to some form or idea or person. We feel the need to trust in something or someone, but this is limited and does not include the rest of life. Until we come upon a direct insight into life, which is real knowing, we can only trust in opinions or what we are told. We merely follow the opinions given to us as we were growing up, or later follow the opinions that make some sense, and these opinions form the basis of our subconscious assumptions about life and the many judgements we make. The mind is always comparing 'this' with 'that' and judging one to be right and the other wrong. These are simply opinions. We never really know for certain about anything unless we experience it ourselves.

We have probably all experienced the herd instinct. This is when we gather together in our small groups and feel exclusive towards others. We often join a group or follow a teaching because we want to be part of something or feel the need to agree with others. We are all searching for something greater of which we can be a part and so we find groups and mass opinions to follow. In order to come into real brotherhood, we have to awaken our own conscience. The herd instinct does not require any real consciousness or conscience, because one can merely follow the group. If we can awaken our own conscience and come into a direct insight of life, then we may come upon a higher, spiritual brotherhood, where we have a deep love for all humanity and all life on the planet. Here we realise our deep connection with everything.

From this level we are able truly to help others, because we can understand them with compassion.

Spiritual groups are useful in leading us into true brotherhood, not one brotherhood from another, but One Brotherhood of Man in the Fatherhood of God. There will always be different groups, but we must be careful not to feel exclusive or more important than others. The group provides the necessary circumstances for direct insight and it gives us an opportunity to serve something greater than our individual selves. As we give ourselves to the group a transformation of energies takes place, and we are in turn fed by the group. As we serve the group, the group serves us. If there is no visible group for us to be a part of, then at least we can meet with friends in the recognition of the One Essence.

The value of group work cannot be overstated. Many people think transformation can be done alone, by reading enough books or attending weekend workshops. Some want to be individualistic and shy away from groups, while others join the first group that comes along offering group support and group opinions. It is certainly difficult to find a group that does not impose itself upon the individual and manipulate everyone to think and act the same way. A real spiritual group, or school, does not impose itself upon the individual, but provides a place of service and an opportunity for transformation. It leads us to freedom, not entrapment. It leads us to the knowledge of who and what we are. The function of a teacher is to bring each person to their own beginning and then to release them. He or she reflects the truth, cutting through the illusions. The purpose of it all is to lead us into love. This is the purpose of the group.

When we meet in love there is a recognition and then a response, which begets a whole pattern of music resounding in our soul. The more we can recognise each other the more we can love each other, and we can only really recognise each other when we know something of ourselves. When we can truly know ourselves, we can truly recognise each other in love. The primary work of a group is to bring us to know ourselves and recognise the self in others. We learn to love each other unconditionally, and when there is enough trust the masks finally come down and we meet each other face to face. Then we will see what brought us together. We will understand that the pain of separation which brought us together has melted in the presence of love.

We all need a place to be safe. We need a place where we feel loved. We need a place to go where we are not imposed upon and can be ourselves. In such a place a new vortex can begin. If we can build this kind of vortex, where people feel safe and not imposed upon, it becomes a sanctuary. It becomes a place where we know we are loved.

We build up a vortex of energy through our love and agreement, and through this vortex there is a possibility for transformational work. The vortex sets up a magnetic force field which attracts its own kind, as like attracts like, and thus a spiritual family begins to take shape. From this family many sub-groups are formed, different interests are shared and people eventually merge back into the world to extend this family even more. Soon there is an extended family all over the world.

In establishing the group vortex, a 'being' slowly comes into independent existence. It will grow from a fragile state, mirroring the more fragile parts of our own nature, and move along the path of the agreement made by the group itself. The growth of this being will be directed and shaped by the kinds of agreement made. If the agreement of the group is towards love and openness, then that will be its direction. If the agreement is concerned with particular opinions about other people or any one person, or about a particular method or approach, then the being will grow in that direction, adding even more energy to the opinions of the group.

We need to be careful in the beginning stages of a group. The 'being' is fragile at first and very impressionable. It is important to begin and grow in the right direction, with agreement, with universal knowledge and love in the path of service. The being needs food to grow, so we need to consider the right kind of food. This is the food of our love and sacrifice. It is not a matter of taking from the group, but of giving to the centre. As the individuals give up their tensions, their pain and their concepts, these are redeemed into the light. They are, in a sense, put into the melting pot, the alchemical cauldron, and if there is sufficient heat (the passion and fervour of love), then something new and wonderful is born. This is the process of alchemy in terms of the individual and the group, and the responsibility of this work even involves the reciprocal maintenance of the planet on a global level.

The group 'being', or vortex, can eventually become the guiding light and indeed the food for all those who come in contact with it. This light can be carried to any part of the world and placed on suitable ground, where it will grow in harmony with the original vortex. It is like taking the light from one candle and lighting as many other candles as are waiting to be lit. It is also like a tree or flower producing thousands of seeds, each having the potential for growing wherever they are planted. You can see the importance of the original impulse and how the work that we do can build a vortex of love and light for the generations to come.

Life unfolds from itself, and each being is a unique manifestation of this One Source. For the one who truly knows himself there can be no quarrel with another expression of that Source in whatever name or form. God is One and humanity is one. In the knowledge of this there is the evergrowing need for cooperation and respect. Once we know our identity as one in essence with all others, we will cease to fight and compare one path with another, attempting to prove one way better than the other, or demanding others to believe as we do. Mankind is truly one and each one of us is interrelated in the web of life, as each nerve in the body is interconnected to every other nerve. A reaction in one causes a response in all the others. Whatever we do there is a corresponding and unavoidable reaction throughout the world. If only we could awaken to this every single moment of our lives.

16

Pain

*If we are asleep we cannot see the purpose in life, and
thus cannot see the purpose of suffering.*

For the most part we are motivated by the thought of
getting something for our efforts. This motivation is
the very basis of our economic system. What would
actually motivate us to do anything unless we expected
something in return? Is it possible to live a life asking for
nothing in return? It is certainly rare that any of us give
unconditionally without at least subconsciously wanting
something for ourselves. I remember a Buddhist monk
who would begin every meditation with breathing out
unconditional goodwill to the world. This is the attitude
to develop, but it is very hard to give in our daily lives
without looking for something in return.

We can even see this in spiritual groups. The vast
majority of them are based entirely upon getting something for oneself. Very rarely are they focused upon
service, where those who attend are just asked to give, and
nothing more. This would be real unconditional love. The
reason most groups are focused upon getting something
or attaining something is because people come to them
out of fear. Most people are attracted to spiritual groups
that make them feel important and special. Everywhere
we turn there are people and groups talking about what
they can get out of life, but very rarely do we hear about
those who just want to give to life. We hear a lot about
unconditional love but rarely what it entails.

Most of the time when a person says, 'I love you' to
another, they want something in return. They are really

saying, 'I want you', or 'I want you to . . . ' They want
to get something for themselves. This is the basis of
many relationships and so there are inevitable fights and
struggles. Rarely do two people just give unconditionally
to each other. If they could, imagine what a very beautiful
relationship that would be. Usually there is not enough
trust. There is also a fear that we are not going to get the
love we need.

Maybe we are so concerned about ourselves because we
do not want to suffer. Giving without receiving something
in return might be considered as suffering. 'Conscious
suffering' is the willingness to suffer the consequences of
giving and serving unconditionally. We want to reject this,
however, because it seems to imply a kind of unfairness to
ourselves. But if we look at the lives of the great saints and
prophets, who gave whatever they could for others and the
future of life, they often suffered along the way.

I'm certainly not advocating that you go out and suffer
or do harm to yourselves. I am not saying that service
has to have martyrdom as our goal. But if we are on the
road of unconditional service, we have to accept the fact
of pain, and sometimes even rejection by those whom
we serve. Jesus was a perfect example of someone who
gave unconditionally but was rejected by those whom he
attempted to serve. If we are willing to give our lives to
unconditional service we also have to be willing to bear
the consequences.

Suffering is inevitable if we dedicate our lives to service.
If we work, not for ourselves but for the evolution of
the planet, for the divine plan, we must be willing
to accept whatever arises from that total commitment.
Out of this acceptance and the willingness to bear all
consequences, suffering becomes conscious suffering. For
example, if we meditate upon peace in the world or work
for peace, it initially results in confrontation, not peace. We
think we are creating peace, but instead we are creating
a confrontation because many forces will come up to
oppose that intention. To have peace means a change
in the world, and many people do not want that change.
We can see this in relationships as well. In fact, whatever

we do for good initially brings about its opposite because something will come in to oppose it. If we have the right intention and the right knowledge we can help the world, but we have to accept the inevitable confrontation and the initial struggle. If we persevere through that inevitable suffering, a transformation will eventually come, so we must be consciously willing to go through it.

Most of us do not want to consider this simple fact. It is easier to avoid the whole issue of suffering, while we talk highly of love or pride ourselves in our spirituality. Unconditional love and service is not as glamorous as some like to think. It is not about getting something in return. It is to do with sacrifice and not acquisition. It is to do with becoming empty so that there may be knowledge. It is not to do with trying to acquire knowledge for we cannot acquire real knowledge. We can acquire book 'knowledge' but not real knowledge because real knowledge is given through our own sacrifice in service. It is given through the yearning to serve because there really is nothing else to do. There is nothing else to do but to serve the truth, and in serving the truth we are given the truth. This is where it really begins.

It begins with commitment. Once the commitment has been made we enter a whole new world. Commitment is a great challenge and we are entirely alone in it. It is something we alone have to make. It is said that the knights of the old days would pray on one knee with their swords facing the earth until they reached the point of commitment whereby they could go out to serve God. When you reach the point of commitment in your own hearts to serve life, then you will find the Way, but you alone have to have the courage to face each moment in your commitment. Each of us will be given something to do and this will be unique unto ourselves. When we meet we will recognise that one great commitment within us. Because of our commitment, we can see what conscious suffering is, and in our commitment we will be able to suffer consciously. Then conscious suffering can become an act of joy, just as the pain of a mother giving birth becomes the joy of bringing a new life into the world.

If we truly put ourselves upon this Path, which means a life of service, it is inevitable that there will be suffering. Many times we are asked to give up something of ourselves in order to give to someone else. A perfect example is parenthood. The parents must give something of themselves in order to bring up a new being in the world. It takes a lot of commitment and a lot of work; any parent will tell you this. It does involve sacrifice and suffering along the way, but there is also the joy of being responsible and giving oneself to that role.

From a greater perspective, pain is seen as a temporary condition of this life. Because we have bodies, emotions and thoughts, we are bound to encounter pain. In giving birth to our true self, there will be pain and there will be joy. The pain we feel is the pain of separation, separation from the truth of our being. This is an illusion because we have never been separate and we never will, but until we are conscious of our true nature, until we are completed in self-knowledge, we will feel the pain of separation.

This pain can turn to joy in the flash of a moment, if we can consciously surrender ourselves to the reality behind the veils of our illusions. This is the dying of our illusions, and what remains is the essential truth of our nature. There are, in fact, many, many stages in this, as in the saying, 'There are many deaths along the Way.' In every death there is some suffering, because that part of us does not want to go. It will hold on to the very last moment, until there is a conscious surrender. It is the pain of separation which will lead us to the point of conscious surrender and assimilation into the divine presence. The pain itself can be seen as an integral part of the Path, just as a tree suffers the pain of its pruning. If we can see pain in this way, as a temporary state leading to the joy of completion, then we will not get so caught up in it as it occurs. There are many different states or experiences. Each one is temporary, and the less we identify with them, whether they be painful or wonderful, the faster we can move on.

Along the Way there is bound to be pain. It is inevitable. There are those who can consciously accept and bear it, and there are those who cannot, and ignore or walk away from it. We may come to understand why we have pain and why it is necessary to bring us to the point where we finally surrender. To yearn passionately for God can be extremely painful. There is pain in the realisation that we feel separate and need to know God. There is suffering in our yearning to know God. This is conscious suffering. Every time we yearn for unity and allow a bit of ourselves to die, there is a time of suffering in that letting go because what we let go of wants to hang on. From this surrendering there comes the joy of release and freedom. Eventually everything that is unnecessary will come up to be recognised and redeemed. It wants to be released and returned to its source.

If we are asleep we cannot see the purpose in life, and thus we cannot see the purpose of suffering. Ultimately, all suffering comes from the pain of separation. People often come to me with some kind of ailment or pain. It is not so difficult to alleviate the symptom, but it is much more difficult to see the purpose of that suffering and help the person fulfil what they are here to do. Remember that healing means 'towards wholeness', and so suffering can be seen as the pain of separation yearning for wholeness. To help a person come into wholeness is the function of a real healer. In one sense, the pain is an illusion because we are not separate from wholeness, but in another sense our separation is what actually makes us aware of this need to be whole. The pain helps us look at ourselves and it can lead us into the realisation of wholeness. Pain is the visiting card to ourselves, which is a more positive way of seeing pain.

Whether we hurt our foot on a thorn or grieve the death of someone close, all this is the pain of separation. There is something to learn here, which is that in reality there is no separation. We may feel separate, and this is what really causes the pain, but we must realise that we are not separate from God. We never were and we never will be. Separation is the great illusion. Without this illusion there would be no pain.

When we find somebody in pain we can be with them, not in sentimentality or in identification with their pain, but just be with them and let them know that they are loved. We can hold a person's hand in the knowledge of love and allow that pain to be released. In love we don't need to identify with another's pain, but we don't want to insulate ourselves from each other either. *When we separate ourselves from each other we are separating ourselves from God.* If we find someone who is locked in their own prison of separation, we cannot force them to open the door, but we can offer them understanding and love without judgement. If we judge someone we are putting ourselves into separation. All we can really do is allow life to go on, to let it unfold and be a part of that unfolding.

Jesus taught that if we knew how to suffer we would not suffer. This is quite the opposite of the Christian tendency towards guilt. There is no need to feel guilty about anything. We all make mistakes and the faster we can let them go, the faster we can get on with something better. Some people feel that they should suffer, that it is good or that it is proof of their saintliness or specialness. Suffering often feeds our self-pity, which makes us feel self-important. We put ourselves in a position to feel miserable so that we can feel self-important and call all our friends for attention saying, 'Look at me, how terrible it is for me. Poor me.' This kind of suffering has no use whatsoever, and it will go on until the person realises that he is writing his own book.

Many times we can discover how we cause our own pain by the quality of our emotions, our thoughts and the way we live. We often impose negative emotions and thoughts upon the natural harmony of life. And if we watch our breath we can see how our negativity changes the natural rhythm of the breath. If we watch the breath we can learn many things about ourselves and the way we react in the world. It is through the observation of the breath that we can really come to know our conditioning and it is through the breath that we can make real changes in our lives.

There is a lot of suffering in the world. Some of it is needed and some of it is not. Some of it is necessary in order to lead us to the truth. Some of it is unnecessary, caused by ignorance, greed and selfishness. The earth does not need to suffer as it does. People do not need to starve or kill each other. All of this is caused by a lack of knowledge and a lack of responsibility. It is a waste of life, and wastage is the only sin. Laying blame is not going to help either. It will merely add to the unnecessary suffering.

What we can do first is forgive. Forgive everyone. Forgive your parents, your family and everyone who has ever hurt you. Forgive all the pain in the world and all those who helped cause it. Forgive the past and all the nonsense that has gone on in the name of truth or in the name of God and religion. Forgive yourselves and all the stupid things you have done. Forgive. Forgive in the knowledge that indeed there is forgiveness, because forgiveness is a quality of God. It is already here. We can really only give agreement to it. God is forgiving because God is love, and it is within this love that we can come into completion.

Suffering often arises from expectation. We have expectations for ourselves that we cannot meet or we have expectations for others that they do not meet. Our ego gets hurt and so we suffer, and since the ego is an illusion, suffering is ultimately an illusion. Yet there is an experience of suffering until we can finally die to all the illusion, until we finally give up and surrender.

In the path of transformation there is always something within us that does not want to give in. Consider the analogy of training a wild horse. We have to control the wild passions of the horse without hurting it, and this has to be done consciously, otherwise we are liable to get kicked. In the same way we have to control our own animal passions, so that they can come to be of use for a higher purpose. We don't want to kill our lower passions, just as we don't want to kill the horse, but we need to bring them under control. During the horse's training it fights back and suffers in the struggle, and it continues to suffer until it gives in to the trainer. Then, out of this surrender the suffering ceases. The suffering is inevitable, just as the rose bush suffers at its pruning, but then is brought joy at its fulfilment.

If we are asleep to the truth, we remain in the pain of separation. We cannot see the truth when we are thinking or presuming that we know it all. The first step to being awake is to realise that we are asleep. When we understand this and wish to wake up, there can be another kind of pain, which is that of our intense yearning to know the truth. We realise that we don't know but wish to know. This is good. It can be very painful to discover we are asleep and that we have little control over ourselves, but we will have to experience this pain before we can go beyond it.

The way through suffering is to be more conscious of its nature and purpose, and then to surrender ourselves to God. If we relate it all back to ourselves it just gets worse. If we can allow ourselves to be pruned, knowing that this is needed for the fulfilment of our destiny, then suffering is transformed, we cease to resist change, allowing it to come about in us. As we come to understand the purpose of life we will see suffering in a new light. We will see the pruning and the suffering as an integral part of this life, or a temporary stage in the unfolding of who we are.

What might appear to be suffering at one moment can turn to joy when we realise that life itself is coming to being because of us. We may experience suffering but if we are conscious that this suffering serves a greater purpose, then that suffering may cease to be. It may be transformed into joy when we know we are one with God, and then the pain of separation dissolves into the ecstasy of life itself.

17

Healing

Real healing is to come into wholeness.

The world needs us. There is so much pain, so much suffering, and it isn't just on the physical level because most of the pain is emotional and mental. Accept the fact that you can help. You have something to give. To be allowed to be of service is a great joy. If you really want to help with all of your heart you will surely be given the opportunity. Did not Jesus say in the Bible, referring to his healing ministry, 'These ye shall do and more'?

There are so many people who need help, who need love, who need to know they are loved, which is the greatest healing in the world. So many people long for freedom, and it is up to those of us who have at least tasted this freedom to help heal the pain of the world. The redemptive Spirit of God, which is the true healer, needs to work through a man or a woman. It does not happen without a living human being, and this is why Jesus Christ was necessary in this world. At all times this redemptive Spirit of healing is available to those who are sufficiently empty, receptive and committed to a life of service.

We need courage and bravery to go out into the world and be an instrument of the highest will. We need confidence, which requires wakefulness, because it is only when we are awake that we can have the confidence to know what we are doing. Be awake to your feet on the ground, to your hands touching another, to your whole body and your whole breath. If you have trouble staying awake, persevere to be awake and have the courage to go out and help the world.

The way to begin is just to love. It is as simple as that. Love, and then something good will come about. But it is not a sentimental kind of love. It is a conscious love. It is love in the light of knowledge. The more we know about someone, the more we can help them because we can consider their needs. Love begins with respect. With respect we can come to know the uniqueness of a person and so know how to really serve them in love. Learn to respect first. Consider the uniqueness of that person or that situation, and then you may be granted the knowledge of what is needed and be able to help.

It is of primary importance in healing to have a question. It is very difficult to approach a situation without opinions, which get in the way of a real question. The question is needed in order to receive the answer, but if we have an opinion it gets in the way of the real answer. So often we have an ulterior motive in healing. We want someone to get better and we want them to be healed in the way that we think is appropriate, but that may not be what is really needed. Perhaps they need to be sick for a while. Our motive in healing needs to be purely attuned to the truth and nothing else. We can then be the links between heaven and earth, but we need to be clear and thoroughly grounded. Often we take action without first asking the necessary questions or asking permission. We assume that we know what to do or that we have permission without really asking. We can want to help so much that we either get in the way or end up doing more harm than good.

In any healing work, or with anything we do, we need to always ask the three questions, May I?, Should I?, Can I?. 'May I?' asks, Do I have permission from the first cause, from God? 'Should I?' asks, Is it the right time and the right place? 'Can I?' asks, Am I the right person to do this? If we ask these three questions we will help more and harm less. These questions are invaluable. Ask inside and listen inside. We will hear the answer as long as we are willing to obey the answer. Ask to be of help, to be of service and to do no harm. It is a matter of having permission, in the light of the very important question, 'May I be allowed to be of service?'

Everything we do has far-reaching effects upon other people and the environment. We presume so often that we can do whatever we want without any consequence for the whole. This is complete ignorance, because everything is interconnected and nothing happens without unknowable consequences. Even so-called healers presume. They presume they can do good, when maybe they should get out of the way. We need to have the questions alive with tremendous intensity. We need to ask with all of our heart in complete prayer for the answer. We want to do the right thing. We don't want to make a mistake. We don't want to put our foot in it when it should be somewhere else. This is the kind of attitude that is needed. It is very much a prayer.

It is said that the road to hell is paved with good intentions. We need knowledge to anchor love. People talk about guidance, not understanding that guidance might not be from the highest knowledge possible. It may be coming from a much lower level, and through the laws of attraction people can manifest floating thought-forms that may not be useful for the present day world. The fact is, if our thought isn't purified we project our own ego, which is a conditioning of the past, and get 'guidance' coming back to boost our self-righteousness. So many people under guidance are actually in the hands of fate. Guidance is often a recurring thought-form wanting to manifest through someone. I've known and heard about people being guided to do the most ridiculous things. They think they are being open to some great intelligence, but it is only a wandering thought-form or desire. Find yourself first. Then you will know the difference between fate and destiny.

We need to be grounded in real knowledge and then we will not be open to wandering thought-forms or false guidance. The need for knowledge became apparent to me years ago in my own healing practice, as I found that without it I could not truly be of service. Love without real knowledge is not enough. Once I could admit to my ignorance it changed my life and I had to give up my healing practice for a period of time until I understood. If I had continued, I might have caused more harm than good, though apparently helping people get better. To admit one's ignorance in the face of God is a big and difficult step. To know that you do not know is the beginning of real knowledge.

I remember meeting a man who had 'hot hands', who felt he had the ability to channel energy and heal people. He was a very well-meaning man, but he had no real knowledge. At first he seemed to be doing wonderful things with people, but soon these very same people began having other symptoms and one even ended up in a mental home. The reason for this was that he released certain kinds of energies at the wrong time and in the wrong place. He had certain powers and a good heart, but he didn't have the necessary knowledge to do the right thing. He was being used, in a sense, by forces that were not fully in his control, and this is always dangerous.

Healing is involved with Shamanism to some degree. There are other beings and elemental energies who exist in another world or in a different geometry to the one we normally know. There are various types of these, and some may work against us. This is why the healer needs to be completely grounded and awake. We can surely be sensitive and attuned with higher knowledge while staying grounded and awake. There is no need to go into some kind of 'trance' state. In fact, this can be quite dangerous for us when we are doing the work, because we may become open to the wrong kind of energies. It is really very easy to go into a trance state or channel other beings, but what is it that is coming through? The true healer or teacher needs to be even more awake and grounded, so that only the highest truth is allowed to come through into the work.

Nothing can happen unless the time is right. We can have all the goodwill in the world but, if there is no receptivity in the moment, then whatever we do will be a waste. One person's needs are not necessarily another's. We cannot presume to know what another needs. We cannot apply one generalisation to everybody, because everybody is different, at least to some degree. We need to be sensitive in the moment to know what is right and when to act. This is the beginning of knowledge and from here we can begin to serve.

In order to help bring forth any kind of healing or help bring about real change in the world, not just the appearance of change, we need to be awake to what is sometimes called 'the third force'. Three is really the first number in the relative world, because it takes three to manifest anything. Remember, 'The One creates the two, the two the three, and the three the ten thousand things.' We can see this 'law of three' at work in everything. One way of looking at this is to consider that there is an active force and there is a receptive force, and then there is a third force, often called 'the allowing force', which reconciles these two opposite forces and brings about unity in the world. It could also be called the redemptive Spirit of God.

If 'I' am talking to 'you' or 'you' are listening to 'me', then there can be no real change. Nothing really happens between us. We have to allow the third force to enter, which is what connects us together. If there is a 'me' separate from 'you', there is no change. If we see ourselves as separate, then there is duality and comparison. The third force, the redemptive Spirit of God, cannot exist with comparison. Learn to be awake to this third force. One of the greatest teachers I ever met said, 'Listen to the wind, Reshad. Listen to the wind.' That is all he ever said and left me to contemplate upon it.

If you try to help you'll find that no change comes about unless the third force is present, which is only possible when you are awake to it. You see, until we awaken, we can't help anyone else. We need to be conscious of who and what we are. Unconsciously, we assume that we are this body, this emotion or this thought. Most often we get identified with a concept about ourself and then we think that is who we are. Only when we are conscious can the body, emotions and thoughts become tools in service to life. The first step is to give up what you think you are, because this is just 'thinking'. It is not the real you. This kind of thinking limits us. We have to go beyond the mind, and certainly beyond thinking. As long as we think we are something, we'll be carrying on an illusion and will probably project that illusion onto others.

Energy follows thought, so we have to be careful that we don't project our own thoughts and beliefs upon another human being. We must not underestimate the power of the love and light and the strength in a human being, because God made man and woman in His image. First respect them, and then you may be granted the knowledge of how to help them to their completion. When we come into the Work we have to do something with thought. The secret, of course, is between the in-breath and out-breath. That is the secret. The question is how?

Most of the time we live in a world of illusion about ourselves and those around us. This illusion is based upon the thoughts we have about ourselves and the world. They are the thoughts and opinions that form the conditioned mind, and thus form the pattern of our lives. As long as we hold on to these concepts, whether they are so-called positive or negative, we cannot see or hear the truth as it is given in the moment, and thus we cannot help ourselves nor anyone else.

Suppose that all of this thought were to be healed, or returned to the One Source. How would we live? If all the illusion were healed, what would we hang on to? Illusory thought is not just negative thought. Negative and positive are merely two polarities of the same basic thing, which is thought. Healing positive thought is much more difficult than healing negative thought. A person says, 'This is what I know, this is who I am and this is where it's at.' This kind of thinking is very hard to work with, because that person is so attached to their concepts of what is true.

Real healing is to come into wholeness, which also means that we come into pure thought. As Jesus, in the Apocryphal Acts of John, said, 'I am thought being wholly thought'. Pure thought is without comparison, without judgement. It is the realization of the perfection of God. It is thought coming from the perfect matrix of creation. The food for pure thought is Spirit, and remember that Spirit means breath. Anything else will merely re-feed the illusion of thought being real unto itself. Pure thought allows the matrix of perfection to be born on earth. It is not a thought in judgement or opinion, but pure and receptive to the truth as it wills to manifest on earth. In this pure thought all beings in the whole kingdom of God are being redeemed back to the One Source.

The aim of healing is union. It is union with the divine, with God, with the One Absolute Being, whatever words you want, so that the sense of separation, which causes all disease, is completely gone. That is the aim of healing. Every single person in need of healing is suffering from one basic problem, which is a sense of separation. In appearance it might seem to be a separation from family or friends, but essentially it is a sense of separation from the One Absolute Being. This is what produces disease. If healing is towards union with God, then we can only really help another by helping them to 'die' to the illusion of separation. That is esoteric healing. It is 'conscious death'. All the other paraphernalia and techniques are merely details or vehicles for this.

There are many levels of healing, each one working from different degrees of understanding and each being equal in essence. The kind we know best is the healing of the physical body; yet this is not necessarily to help it get better but to prepare it for death. Healing is not for life. It is for death. This is important, because from the moment we are born we are dying and one day the physical body will have to die. It will have to become compost. That is good ecology! It is even better ecology if we can clear the memory patterns from the cells of a human body before it dies. In that level of healing, there is freedom.

Esoteric healing is helping people to die consciously in every single moment of their lives. It doesn't help people to keep illusion going, an illusion that will have to die one day. Healing is helping the flow of life to continue. We are called upon as healers, in whatever profession, to be an instrument for the healing force of life to flow on, and this leads to eternal life in the knowledge that who we are can never die. This is the real meaning of conscious death, to let go consciously of everything, including the concept of ourselves, and allow the flow of life to live on.

Healing takes less time than the opening and closing of an eye, but we've got to get somebody to that point. Do it with loving kindness. A great man once said to me, 'Love your brother and sister into the present moment.' Once we get someone into the present moment, then it is easy. Remember that real healing is towards wholeness. It is to come back to our true self, which is not separate from the whole of existence. It is to be here completely, with all of our self and all of our love.

Fear is the cause of many of our problems, but of what are we frightened? What I have seen is that people are frightened of presenting their face to the world. Whether it comes from parents or from a cultural neurosis, most people cannot bear the pain of facing the world. They are afraid to be who they are and show themselves in the world. Can you present your face to me? Can you allow me to see you? Can you say, 'Here I am!' Do not be afraid. Be proud of who you are. Know that you are loved. Then there is healing. If you realise that you are the representative of God on earth, you will never again be frightened of presenting yourself. Once you know this you will know what acceptance is. As representatives of God, we are here to show our face in the world and reveal our unique beauty to others. We are here to know we are loved, and so be able to give ourselves without shame or guilt.

It is said that the sole purpose of love is beauty. When we make a flower arrangement we are making each flower beautiful within the overall pattern. It is a matter of respect. We don't just shove flowers into a pot and hope for the best. We are arranging them to present themselves beautifully, and by doing this we are loving the flowers. We are helping them present themselves to the world, revealing their natural beauty.

The greatest healing in the world is to know you are loved. Can you accept that? If you don't know you are loved you will be in a lot of pain, stumbling around the world looking for someone to love you, and it will be very difficult to love someone else. If you can see how important this is for everyone, you will have a lot more compassion for people. You will meet people and see that they are frightened and need to know they are loved. So respect every single person you meet and help them know they are loved. When someone comes to know they are loved, there is a release of energy for the whole world, and the angels sing on high.

18

Prayer

True prayer is an act of total self-giving.

Life is a prayer, and until we understand this we are merely puppets in this world, moved by the strings of the collective unconscious and our own conditioning. To know that life is a prayer is to realise a great possibility in life. What do you want? Ask yourself what you want from life. Probably a whole flood of ideas come to mind, but what do you really want in the depths of your heart? Do you want to know the truth? Do you want union with God? That's a big prayer indeed, but it is fully possible if we are willing to go for it. Prayer does work, or at least it allows the answer to come, but we have to hold that one great prayer in our heart. It has to come from the heart. We have to know it in the heart and we have to feel it in the heart. It is like a burning question, or the burning prayer, Mevlana's 'burning, only burning'.

We each have the free choice to ask the question or not ask the question. Either we affirm that prayer or forget it. Either we realise our dependence upon God and ask for what we need with all our heart, or we're on our own. Whatever we ask for, it is a legitimate prayer if it comes from a sincere need or yearning. Prayer is the expression of a need, on one level or another, of something that appears to be unattainable without some kind of greater help. And if the prayer is for union with God, then it needs to resound continuously in our hearts.

This is the way to live. It is a life full of passion, the passion to know and be one with God. It is a beautiful way to live and I can't imagine any other way myself.

If we are lucky enough to meet up with another human being who has touched this fire and who is burning in prayer for God, then we'll see that it doesn't matter what religion we have or what group we belong to, because that person has found the flame and can light the spark in our own heart. Life is a prayer, and we are that living prayer.

We could say that prayer is to communicate with God. God is not something out there, outside of ourselves. Rather, there is One God in all things. Whatever image we have of God, however different from another's, it is in fact only a different manifestation or reflection of the One Eternal Truth. There is One Absolute Being from which all emanates and to which all returns. We can pray in God, where there is no separation between us and God, between creator and creature. This is where the individual meets the eternal essence. When we enter the world of pure essence we enter that which is already perfect. We affirm the ever-living presence and deny anything but the unity. This is prayer in the realisation of unity, which leads all awareness back to the ocean of essence. We do not pray to God, but we pray in the knowledge of unity, knowing that without that One Prayer things will not come about. This is hard for the mind to understand. There is One Absolute Being. God is not somewhere distant from us. The future of this world depends entirely upon the affirmation of this One Being, without which the experiment of mankind on earth will not succeed.

There are three basic sorts of prayer. The prayer of ignorance is when we pray for something without considering the consequences. It is wanting or asking for things without realising that 'you cannot pick a flower without the troubling of a star'. Is what we ask for something that we really need? Is it only for ourselves? Second, there is what I call the prayer of duality, which is asking God to intercede in the world in some way. This is a Christian form of prayer as in, 'Father, please help me be a better person,' or, 'Almighty God, may we have peace in our time?' The third form of prayer is prayer in unity, which is on a different level. Prayer in unity is possible when we have surrendered everything of ourselves into unity and thus nothing else exists. When we realise our unity within the One, then we can pray within the unity. Every time we affirm the unity of God in the complete knowledge of this, someone in the world is yearning towards unity.

'Being in unity' does not mean that we think we are God, because this would limit God. Instead, we realise in humility that God lives through us, and prayer in unity is dependent upon the degree of this awareness. If we are not humble, we cannot be the agents through which God works. God is the only knower and God is the only doer, and prayer in unity is the affirmation of this essential unity. At the highest level of prayer we do not need to ask for anything because everything is already complete, and we know we are given exactly what we need to fulfil our part in the divine plan if we can willingly accept it.

If we say within, 'I will', knowing that in this sacrifice we come to be merged in the great ocean of love, then whatever is necessary at this moment in time will come to pass. There is a vast hierarchy of divine helpers at different levels of consciousness, each with a specific function in order that God's will may manifest in this world. Everything happens within consciousness and within prayer. Manifestation requires the help of many invisible beings on many levels, and it requires our help and our prayers. We become the agents for this divine plan to work itself out. Within unity we each have a unique job to do for the will of God to be made manifest. We therefore need knowledge, the knowledge of ourselves and of God's will, because the greater our knowledge the more perfect our prayer. Then we will know the power of prayer.

Prayer is an exercise of the will, in which the created human will seeks loving identification with the will of God. It is a personal encounter with the divine will. This is the height of prayer. No more is there 'you' trying to get what you think you want, or trying to help others get what you think they should have. All opinion goes out the window, and all we want to do is serve God's will. There is no other intention.

We need to develop a personal communication in prayer or invocation. Thoughts without feelings are useless, and feelings without thoughts are equally useless. Without feeling we are only half alive, and without a question we are only half here as well. A question brings prayer to life, and through the question you may have a response. When we say, 'May I be allowed to be of service this day', we are asking a question. We are asking to be a part of the work of transformation. If we have a question in our prayers it makes the prayer alive.

Prayer is to give God the undivided attention of a lover. True prayer is an act of total self-giving, and a vehicle for sacrifice. Praying for someone is not a matter of holding that person in a certain concept of being well, but is a willingness to sacrifice ourselves for that person. When we can sacrifice ourselves for another we are giving something of love and healing to them. It is not a matter of projecting energy or performing magic. It is to do with giving ourselves so completely that we surrender our whole life in that moment of sacrifice.

In the Kabbala there is the 'lightning flash', which comes down from above into the world of manifestation. This can be seen as the grace of God or the rain from heaven descending on earth. Yet we cannot just rely upon this grace. There is something we must do. Evolution is dependent upon man and woman, and it is prayer that spirals evolution. We could say that God has His job to do and we have ours. There is a descent of purified forces into this world, but the manifestation of this on earth is dependent upon man and his ability to produce what we call 'conscious evolution'. In prayer we become the vehicles for God's will on earth. Through prayer we become the creator, though there is the One Creator beyond. Then we can actually do something. The correct attitude in humility brings us to a state of being, which can be seen as the preparation to prayer. That is when there is no separation between myself and my Father, as in the saying of Jesus, 'I and my Father are one.' In this knowledge we can truly be of service.

Our prayers help towards conscious evolution. Every step we make in our sacrifice helps the unfolding of God's plan. We must continually remember that we are not doing the Work, but the Work is being done through us. We are not developing ourselves, because that would be a further development of the illusion of ourselves as separate from God. Instead, remember that as you sacrifice yourself for the Work, you become a more purified instrument for its unfoldment. It is not a matter of developing what we think we are, but sacrificing the illusions of what we think we are and allowing the unfolding to take place through us. It is an entirely different attitude to what we are usually taught in the West. Every step taken in conscious evolution requires something to be given up. We have to pay for everything in this world. And every time we give up a little bit of the illusion of our separation and take a step in service to the work, we are allowing that lightning flash of God's will to come on earth. This is a great responsibility.

We can allow the Spirit to infuse us, which can be seen as a fusion of the higher nature with the lower, the Spirit with the body. It is a spiritualisation of matter and a crystallisation of light energy. In this way we become a vessel for the Spirit to enter. So, we need to live at a higher rate of vibration, because the lower vibrations, or identifications, block out the fullness of the spiritual light. We need to let in the Spirit and work with it, which means working with will, because will and Spirit go hand in hand. With will we can allow more Spirit to enter through us and through the planet.

Put yourself into an active receptive state so that you are prayed through. When we are in such a state of prayer, whatever needs to be prayed for will come forth for help. We are in a state of readiness to serve whatever comes up, and it could be someone we know or it could be something going on across the world. We just give ourselves up to be a pure vehicle for prayer. Don't underestimate yourselves. There is much that can be done on an inner level, but it's not a matter of imposing what we think is right upon that situation. In prayer we are not making something happen, but allowing what is needed to happen by being an opening for divine grace to enter in the way that is needed. It is prayer that spirals evolution, and it is prayer that brings about real change, not the appearance of change.

Whatever is happening in each of our lives is being reflected to some extent in the world at this very moment. Walls cannot divide us, and when we can accept this responsibility we are at the beginning of the Way. The world is truly here within this space, and all that we can do for good, or for God, is dependent upon the degree of our realisation. If we can breathe in harmony with the universe, then amazing things will happen.

We have to accept the responsibility of being human beings on this planet. Whatever we think about another person, or how we judge the world, or what we want out of life, starts to bring about a manifestation. A thought-form never dies, until it is redeemed back through man. Our bodies are a combination of fire, earth, air and water, and these elements are ultimately at our command. Our thoughts and prayers are indeed powerful, and this is why we need to be even more careful as we go along the Path, because when the command is given, the elements in that combination are locked into that decision and they cannot get out of it, until they are redeemed through man. So we have to be awake. Think of all the people in the world who are asleep and not in control of their thoughts. They are not consciously thinking, but are being used by thought, and all the chaos and violence in the world is just a manifestation of these unredeemed thought-forms locked into their destination. This is why the work on ourselves is so very important, because we are transforming energies.

We cannot pray if we are asleep and we cannot get the answer if we are asleep when it comes. We must be conscious and actively engaged in the prayer. Consciousness can be defined as the reaction of active intelligence to pattern. This pattern is the perfect geometry of God, or the divine order, which permeates all life and manifests itself through the many planes of consciousness. Some say that there are at least twelve spheres, or dimensions, each having its own particular geometry and laws, which we can consciously pray through. Mystical prayer is rising through the spheres to 'break beyond the sky', going beyond dimension, then bringing back through the vortex pure Spirit into this world. We could also say that it is the quickening of the Spirit into this world.

We must be conscious so that this action can manifest through us, and in order to be conscious we must activate our innate intelligence through will. Our intelligence lies dormant until we awaken it through will, which means that we must first want to awaken it. It isn't activated just by itself without work; it doesn't just *happen*. We don't just wake up one day intelligent. We must work on it; we must work on waking up. This is the beginning of knowledge through the awakening of our intelligence. It is the knowledge of pattern, the knowledge of divine order and the interconnectedness of all life. When we are in this knowledge then we can call ourselves conscious beings. Our aim, therefore, in prayer, is to surrender, as conscious lovers of the Beloved, into the redemptive Spirit of God through which all miracles come. Within God's will is perfect order, and the manifestation of God's will on earth brings about the order that is necessary for the reciprocal maintenance of the planet.

In order to receive the answer to our prayers, or in order to know what we are meant to do, we need to attune ourselves to that answer. Breath and silence are essential to this attunement. But we also have to 'be here' to receive the answer. Since the answer is really already here, we can only receive as much of it as we are here to receive. Just about the time we get bored or go to sleep, the answer appears. We have to put more and more effort into staying awake, and that means to be fully here and present. We need to bring our full attention to this moment, and we need fully to inhabit our body.

If we want to receive the answers to our prayers or our questions, then we have to inhabit the vehicle through which the answer may come. God made us in His image. The only ears God has are ours, and the only mouth He has is ours. Part of my work has been to wake people up and help them get here. In order to receive knowledge we have to get here, and in order to apply knowledge we have to be here. We can never receive anything really, unless we are here, and we can never really do anything, unless we inhabit this body and are awake to the present moment.

In prayer, we need the right attitude and intention set deep into the flesh itself. It is no good having a wishy-washy attitude that is up in the air. We have to get it down into the actual flesh. We have to feel it in the body. It is essential that we come to realise that this body, this vehicle made up of its many parts, is the vehicle from which we pray and through which our prayer is answered, even if the prayer appears to be answered from the outside. Let us pray for guidance all the time, that we be guided on the straight way. Someone on the Way may be giving the answer, but if we are not awake we will not get the answer. When we pray we need to be awake, not only to pray but also to get the answer.

The answer is not really outside ourselves, but because we cannot find it inside ourselves, God produces the mirror outside so that we can see it inside. When the Sufis talk about polishing the mirror, it doesn't just mean for ourselves, it means for God. If I polish my mirror, you may get the answer you need through me, and if you polish your mirror, I may get the answer I need through you. Polishing the mirror is an act of surrender, sacrifice and responsibility for God and humanity. If we see something 'outside' it may be coming in answer to our prayer, because we cannot see it all 'inside'. The answer will come dependent upon the condition we are in when we are praying.

Being in a higher state of prayer we need not worry about seeing or hearing the answer. It may not be the right time for the answer, or we may not be the right person to hear it. This state of prayer is not limited to just receiving the answer, because the prayer comes from beyond you. The answer is not for you alone and may not be for you at all. In this prayer we can ask, but there is nothing else that we can do. Sometimes the answer comes quickly, while at other times the answer takes a long time to manifest. It depends upon the need and upon the movement through the higher worlds into this one.

If we pray for ourselves or pray out of self-pity, the prayer is of a lower vibration than if we pray for others or pray from a very deep question in our heart. There are different rates of vibrations to which we resonate. The lowest is apathy, at which there is very little Spirit at all. Then comes self-pity, where we are closed to anything coming in, because we are so wrapped up in our own pain. In self-pity we cannot hear or see anything, and in fact we begin to resent what could actually help us. The next is fear; in fear we tighten, or block out, what is coming in. In all of these states, which we all experience to some degree or another, we are trapped in the illusion of our own separateness, so the Spirit can only enter to a limited extent. In order to be free of these lower levels of vibration we need to be free of our self-identification, which closes us off from Spirit entering.

We raise the rate of vibration by praying for understanding or to be of service. In this way we raise ourselves up from apathy, self-pity or fear, but the moment we turn our attention back onto ourselves we go back into these lower states. We need to come into a greater intention and a pure motive. We raise our rate of vibration by ceasing to identify with these states, just as in some forms of meditation one practises observation of the mind without identification. The highest vibration is 'the still centre', because in this stillness of being there is unlimited energy and a freedom of consciousness.

This is where prayer and meditation come close to being the same. In meditation we come into the true nature of our being, which is not separate from any other being. In both meditation and prayer we need to consider our intention. Are we after power for ourselves? Are we trying to attain something for ourselves, or are we intending to be of service to a greater cause and willing to be transformed along the way? The true intention for both meditation and prayer should be love, for love is the cause and effect of all creation. We say, 'God is love, the lover and the beloved.' Mevlana said, 'Love alone is capable of revealing the true nature of love and of being a lover.' True prayer must come from love. We need to be able to relax into this love and trust in its natural flow. We need to realise that love is the cause of all creation, and love will flow where it is needed when we ourselves have surrendered to it.

19

Unity in God

Oh Lord, take away the I that stands between Thee and me. BISTAMI

We may finally come to a point in life when, in knowledge, we cease to exist separate from God. Everything turns inside out and we see that we were never separate from God, never at all. God is One and contains every part and all the elements that make up the whole. The universe finds its reflection and perfection in man and woman, who potentially contain the pure distillation of all the elements. It is as Mevlana said: 'I died as a mineral to become a plant, I died as a plant to become an animal, I died as an animal to become man.' Within this 'I' there are different steps in the distillation of the heart, until man loses his own heart completely in the heart of God. That is why it is said, 'The Gnostic has no heart'. We have to die to become Gnostics. We have to lose our hearts to God. We have to give up our hearts, until we are nothing but an empty centre, and within that empty centre is the greatest knowledge in the universe.

The child wanting food cries and cries, because of a need. That need is real. As we grow up into responsible human beings our need is not for our mother and her milk, but for God's love and knowledge. Our food is knowledge, but unless we know that we need knowledge and want it very much, that food will elude us. We do not turn towards that food unless we become as a child needing it, as in the saying of Jesus, 'Become as little children'. Nothing will ever satisfy the soul, except for knowledge, the knowledge of God and the knowledge of love. This is the attitude to have in prayer. Be completely dependent on the One Absolute Being. When we know there is only One Absolute Being, we are still dependent, but in freedom as well. In this freedom we can help bring others into freedom, which is a tremendous joy.

The only possibility of freedom is by dissolving into the unity of God through knowledge. But unity will only be fully realized when all mankind turns to unity. That is the degree of sacrifice we are asked to make. There is much to be gained in this knowing, but not for ourselves alone. What is gained is freedom, freedom for the world and freedom for the children of the world, who are the new teachers arriving every moment.

We need to affirm the truth and sacrifice anything other than the truth. There are many ways to affirm the unity of God, which is testifying to our own unity within God, but we must first say 'No' to any form of separation. First there is the denying, the complete denying of anything separate from God. God is not separate from us, but we have to let go of all the concepts we have of ourselves and of God. First realize that you do not know yourself, and you do not know God. What one thinks about God is not God. We are saying 'No' to all separation and to all concepts limiting the truth. We are denying any conception of an outer world as separate from God.

The world we live in is not separate from the unity of God. Even the concept of the inner world must go. Some will say, 'I will find God within', but this is as much an illusion as is finding God only in the outer world. Within and without are nothing but concepts of the mind; they are illusions. Some look for God up there, some look down here. Some think that God came and went some time in the past, while others think God will arrive one day in the future. Whether it is in, out, up, down, yesterday or tomorrow, it is a form of duality created in the mind. The mind needs this duality or it cannot really exist. The mind is a wonderful expression of God's truth, but in remembrance we surrender that duality. We say 'No'. We are not interested in these concepts. God is beyond any concept or any form, beyond the mind and even beyond consciousness.

No one has ever described God. No one has ever been able to say who or what God is. No one can ever say 'this' or 'that' is God. Someone may point out a manifestation of God, something of His beauty, His majesty, His light, His power; but no one can point out God. No man or woman can touch God. No man or woman can see God. We cannot really talk about God at all. But we can love, and we can participate in the presence of God through His manifestations. This is not something we do for ourselves alone, and it is not something we do for somebody else alone, because there is only One Absolute Being.

The bird sings in the tree calling out its own space, defining its own space. The ocean roars, and defines its space. The thunder cracks and lightning flashes in the sky. This is defining space. It is all about praising God because as creation becomes known, God is praised. We are here to praise God by knowing God in creation. Man and woman are the only creatures of God who can consciously know and express the unity of God. When we remember the unity we are no more defining our own small space like the bird. Instead, we are denying all limitation and separation, while consciously affirming the unity, which is all space and all time, and which is already complete. We are affirming the unity and sounding the space of unity.

The use of sound is very ancient in esoteric practice. It is very powerful in the work of transformation, because sound creates pattern, the pattern of our lives. The real sound is in the question. It is in our longing to know God, to come into unity with the source of life itself. Remembrance of God is something for us to understand in our own way. Do it in your own way. Remember God in your own life and in every moment you are awake. Through this remembrance you free God.

To free God is to free the love in each other and to help each other be free in love, as in Mevlana's saying, 'Love is known only by those who become lovers.' There is one great purpose for which we are here, and I leave you this as a question. I am not going to tell you what the answer is.

That is for you to live. That question is your living prayer, and what that sound is for you will be your own.

Our lives should be a prayer. My life is a prayer. We may pray in the same way, but inside it is our own sound, and that sound is literally our love of life. Can you hear the sound of your love? The sound is the same in essence, but each person resounds a different sound. Each resonates that sound in a different way. Without a question we are not really alive. We may presume to be alive and we may presume to know all the answers, but what is the point of being alive if you think you know all the answers? So, be alive within the question of your life. This is prayer.

Living prayer is a continuous flow of the essence, and this can only come about when we no longer exist separate from God, so that in every breath there is only God. Yet, we cannot expect to be in continuous remembrance. This is way beyond us. It is approaching sainthood. What we can do is aim to live life in total spontaneity so that we can go from one situation to another, doing whatever we need to do at any one moment. At first there is no real possibility of spontaneity because we are in so much pain, and we are running around trying to get out of that pain. We hang on to anything that makes some sense to us, but are not capable of seeing the root from which all things come.

We have to be able to serve the moment without any hesitation, but our conditioning keeps us from being spontaneous. Our conditioning veils us from the pure awareness we need in order to see what is needed and respond without hesitation. Spontaneity is something we can learn, not by following a belief system, but by doing whatever is needed in the moment. Spontaneity can bring about emptiness. If we can act spontaneously without thinking of ourselves, then eventually there will be nothing left of ourselves but service. This is where prayer or remembrance begins. It begins by emptying ourselves of ourself, so that eventually there is nothing but God. Then we are spontaneously manifesting that which is precipitating itself from eternity. We are testifying to the truth manifesting in the moment, and this is remembrance.

The ultimate realization is that there is only one moment which unfolds throughout time, and the world comes into being in this one moment of time. Creation is coming into being and passing out of being every moment. Creation is in one moment, the present moment. If we could realize this, we would know that all possibility exists right here now. Allow yourselves to become still in this moment. Take in a breath, a conscious breath, then release it into eternity. There is no time but now. If we are conscious in the breath we can know what this means.

Creation does not come out of this world. A rapture comes upon a human being when he or she has the extraordinary experience that there is no creation in this world at all, there is only the becoming of being. If we can realize this we will come upon the ecstasy of knowing that there is only One Being. This is the ecstatic knowledge of unity.

It is possible that we can all reach this state of ecstasy. We are all longing for someone or something to lead us back to unity, and Sufism is often called the path of return. It is the path to unity. We need a way through the eye of the needle. As Mevlana said, 'Come, come, whoever you are, wanderer, worshipper, lover of leaving, it doesn't matter. Ours is not a caravan of despair. Come, come even if you have broken your vow a thousand times, come, come yet again, come.'

Ecstasy is like the ripping of the veil that stands between us and God. The Sufi Bistami said, 'Oh Lord, take away the I that stands between Thee and me.' Without this, the Path is just words. Ecstasy is the breaking open of the heart, and once it happens we can never go back. It can happen very quietly. It doesn't have to be explosive. Ecstasy is not a concept of the mind. It is not an emotional jumping up and down. It is an inner fire that burns.

Maybe you have experienced times of ecstasy, to some degree at least, sitting in a church, looking at the sky or out onto an incredible view. The heart opens and you are completely in love, without any comparison to anything else. You melt into the very essence of life itself. Look at the stars, at the incredible depth of this universe upon universe, sounds upon sounds. People are frightened of this depth. It's so vast and incomprehensible. It is overwhelming. But that's what is so incredible. People are terrified of ecstasy, of letting go into the power of this vast depth. They're terrified of an ecstatic madness, or maybe of the inevitable transformation, like a crysalis turned into a butterfly. Ecstasy can bring us to madness or revelation, and what protects us from madness is brotherhood and service.

Ecstasy is not a matter of pleasing anyone or performing correctly according to some prescribed form. How we express the power in our hearts is a very personal thing, and it doesn't matter whether we are Christian, Jew, Muslim, Buddhist or atheist. It simply doesn't matter. Ecstasy is something very powerful and very strong, but also very private. If we express ecstasy we need to be responsible for that expression but not be frightened by that expression.

Ecstasy is even necessary in the Way. I can't create ecstasy, and neither can you. It is a gift. We can work towards it and make a step towards it. We have to take the first step towards God and He will take ten steps towards us. But don't be frightened of ecstasy, because you never know what will happen. Don't worry about when it will come or how it will express itself. It may explode through you while making love, or out hiking or gardening, but don't think of it in terms of anything in particular. Making love is allowing God to make love in us, and that is the greatest ecstasy of all.

We can walk around the streets of cities anywhere and see 'dead' people who have lost the passion for living. They are longing for ecstasy but do not know it. Maybe they do not know it is possible, or maybe they have given up and even forgotten. Or maybe they just don't care anymore. People are walking around in a lot of pain, and ultimately it is the pain of separation. I look around sometimes at the complete disillusionment—people completely lost, with nothing but their own pain, their fears and guilts—a great disaster. They are terrified of ecstasy.

Do not be afraid of ecstasy. This is very important. Every single person has within them the yearning to burst out in ecstasy. Don't make it up. Don't mimic others or let others tell you what it is or how to get there. Don't shout out praises or sing lovely prayers if you don't believe them. If it is not real for you, don't believe it. But don't be afraid of expressing ecstasy or joy. Don't be afraid of the out-breath, because there is no other way to die except on the out-breath. We are so inhibited. We have fear and guilt about so many things that we don't understand what it is to breathe out completely. When we can let it all go there is ecstasy. We all yearn for this.

Mevlana came into the ecstatic rapture of love, which I pray you will come into at some point. He turned around and around in love, and only he knew that he was expressing the movement for the next cycle of mankind. He turned and turned towards union. He was moving to the point of union where there is no more separation. This is when you finally know without any doubt that God is One and there is no other. One day there will be no more wars, no more fighting, because there will be an understanding of the purpose of life on earth. There are people all over the world who long to be free, and all of these people are part of you. Everybody has this longing deep within their, the yearning to know they are loved. We yearn for freedom in love. I pray that you too will one day become free in love.

20

The Substance of Being

To live the spiritual life is to allow the eternal to manifest in the moment without distorting it with the illusions of what we think it is.

Life is a natural thing. We wash, we eat, we sleep, we make love. It is all very natural. But if we are asleep to these natural things, then our life is a waste of time. Be grateful for this life, and then you can be proud to be alive. Then you can serve life. How ridiculous it is to try to find God other than here. It is abnormal. How ridiculous it is to try to be spiritual and forget how to be natural. Think of our children, who are joyful about life, who are not trying to be spiritual or to be anywhere else other than just here. What a nonsense it is to neglect that which is. To be natural is to be proud and joyful for all that we are given. It is all here, and it is up to us to see it.

Be proud to be alive. It is not a matter of feeling special. We can be proud just to be alive and have this great possibility of conscious life. It is actually very normal, but we forget what we are given in this extraordinary adventure of life. We are not special, yet we can be proud of having this wonderful opportunity and using it for all that it is worth. Life is worth everything. We may make mistakes, but we all make mistakes, and if we are honest about this then others will not be hurt, but will learn as we learn. Life is an extraordinary adventure in which we can participate. When we wake up to this, then we can be proud to be alive.

Now is the time when the spiritual path has to come right into life. The world needs us. God needs us. The teaching of this time is for man and woman to become conscious and responsible for the whole of creation. This is what we are asked to do and need to do, and it is the most exciting adventure in the world. The spiritual life is not separate from the world. It is not an escape from life. The natural life is the same as the spiritual life, because both mean being one with the flow of life itself. There is a flow of life right now in this moment. The divine is pouring into the world according to the needs of the moment, and all things are an expression of the divine realizing itself.

To live the spiritual life is to allow the eternal to manifest in the moment without distorting it with the illusions of what we think it is. We can serve this manifestation and fulfil our purpose as human beings. We can turn towards that One Source of all life and open ourselves in love, so that life can flow freely through us and in the world. This turning and opening in love is the meaning of prayer, as we relax into the One Being and allow the Love of God, or the will of God, to flow where it is needed. This is the essential yearning of the human being, who can be the purified vehicle for Love to enter the world.

You see, being spiritual does not mean we have to go off to a cave and meditate. To be spiritual is not to be separate from life. Whatever we choose to do can be in service to the Work, as long as we are willing to be responsible for ourselves and each other. The world needs us, but we can't do everything ourselves. Each of us can have a very special role to play, if we work hard to develop our talents and offer them up to God. Find a way to make yourself useful, and ask every day that you may be allowed to be of service. We can all be parents of a new age, which is to bring forth divine possibility into manifestation, and the way that we can do this is to be conscious and responsible to the needs of the moment.

We cannot ask that we reap the benefits of our work. What we plant today will be harvested when the time is right. We may never see the complete results. It is only the illusion of our self that demands to see the results. The sacrifice we make today may result in a great joy for someone else tomorrow. It doesn't really matter that we reap the benefits or not, because, in reality, there is no separation between us. There is only God.

The spiritual work is not glamorous. It does not mean we have to wear crystals or robes, have special mantras, see auras or channel ascended masters. This is all very lovely, but it is not what the spiritual path is about. What it is about is the transformation of ourselves and being of use in the world. It does not mean being anything other than being in this world. We are asked to be here because we are here. Why would you be here if there wasn't something for you to do?

There is something for everyone to do. We each can fulfil some function in the overall divine work. Everyone can play a part, and each is equally important. We all can't go around the world teaching. Somebody has to make shoes. Somebody has to clean bathrooms. It is all equal in the eyes of God. It is all spiritual if it needs to be done, because there are many things that need to be done and somebody has to take it on. This is the functional aspect of the Work. One function isn't any better than another. We do what we can, and, I hope, we do it to the best of our abilities.

There is something else that can come into this and that is called 'being'. Being is what we can possibly put into our work. It is like a substance that can enter into anything we do, depending upon our degree of consciousness at the time. We are like a chalice holding the spirit of life. What we can give is dependent upon our capacity and this is dependent upon our degree of emptiness. If we can be like the chalice, empty and giving all the time, then we can have the capacity for Spirit to enter through us and into whatever we do, or whomever we meet. Being has to do with capacity, and it comes about through consciously giving ourselves totally to whatever we do in the present moment.

Being is a divine substance, which can manifest through anything. It is something of the infinite that we can work with and be able to manifest. Consider the bee. A bee goes from place to place and gathers pollen. Then a very remarkable thing happens. Not only does the bee produce honey out of the nectar of flowers, but it also produces the substance for building its own house, which is geometrically perfect. So the bee produces food and the perfect shape for its own existence. It also goes about and cross-pollinates the flowers. It therefore serves its environment. The bee is truly remarkable, but what about human beings? Can we participate in similar acts of transformation? Those of us in the way of love are asked to do consciously what the bee does by instinct. In fact, the Way is built by people of the Way. We are transformers of subtle energies. We take in food from our meals, from the air we breathe, and from the impressions we consciously receive. From these foods and the sacrifice we make, we produce a refined alchemical substance which travels with us and spreads out into the world, and it goes on and on. The Way is within us and it unfolds itself through us.

This substance could be called the soul. The soul is a dimensionless point. What we are is a dimensionless point. It is not very romantic and it doesn't make us very important. It's just who we are, and it goes on forever. If we truly want 'to die before we die', which is the only way to release the illusion of what we think we are and come to know who we really are, then we have to surrender everything of ourselves to this dimensionless point. This is true freedom. Surrender yourself into the dimensionless point, from which all things come and to which all things go. We have to give everything up and die completely into the one point which has no dimension. This one point, which is not even a point, is unlimited, and there is unlimited possibility of what can come about through it. It needs to be turned into 'dimension' for the reciprocal maintenance of the planet. It is first dimensionless, then it has a point, and from there it has the definition we give it. We extend it from point to point to make a line, and from there we can make the patterns of life. That is the possibility, the infinite possibility of man and woman.

The application is simple. Some of you may become doctors, some architects, some carpenters, some gardeners, some will run schools and some will teach children. The application is incredibly simple if you can remember that when you put a spade into the earth, when you touch a child or a friend, that 'knowing substance' can be shared and extended. A line can be drawn from the dimensionless point to another being or to the work you do, and through this a new pattern is made manifest upon the earth as you extend the golden thread of knowledge, the substance of the soul.

Picture a child holding a lighted sparkler in the night sky. He can draw a picture or make circles with it. He can make a line and then a triangle. He can make any pattern he wants as long as that little sparkler is kept alight. He can even memorize that pattern for the rest of his life. He can pass that pattern on to his children, and the children could pass it on to their children, and it could go on through generations and generations. The substance of the soul is like the substance of the sparkler. It can literally move out of non-dimension and into dimension. Isn't this the work of any architect? The architect takes the dimensionless point at the end of his pen and creates dimension, the expression of something being brought into play. You may not be an architect, but you are able to do the same thing. You are the pens of God. You are the pen that draws the line of your life.

Wherever you go, realize that you are the pen of God, you are that sparkler in the night sky. This is the responsibility of being born. That is the beginning of the Work. It is not the end, but the beginning. When you know this you can hold hands or touch one another with the understanding that this substance is brought forth and exchanged. When you dance, or make music, you can see, like the child with a sparkler in the night sky, the whole pattern being played. You can even see beyond the form and see the substance within the form. Then you can thank God that this vehicle exists, just as the pen exists for the lines and patterns to be drawn from the substance, which is given for us to use. Realise that the pen is here for the ink and the ink is here for the patterns to be made. Realise that it all happens through you, if you are awake. You are the pen through which the ink may flow.

We can all make use of this substance, but first we need to have it. We can all put more of our full 'being' into whatever we do, and there is always more to give, but we need to have being before we can give it. Our spiritual being needs to grow, and in order for it to grow we need three foods: the food we eat—which is dependent upon what is in it, the quality of its preparation and the way we eat it—the air we breathe, and the impressions we receive. This is the food for being. And we are responsible for providing this food. We are responsible for feeding our bodies healthy food, for consciously breathing a higher quality of air, and for receiving needed impressions.

All human beings need impressions, but rarely do we consider how to receive impressions and use them for the development of our being. There is an art to receiving impressions. If we go about our lives unconsciously or asleep to the food of impressions, then our being is not properly fed and we have little to give, if anything. Any impression which is based upon comparison is food for the mind, but not for the being. If we can receive impressions without comparison, which requires us to have what is called a 'permanent observer', which can receive impressions without judgement, then we can acquire food for being. Being does not live by comparison. It can only live without comparison, which is to recognize the unique qualities and forms of life for what they are, not in comparison to what we want them to be.

We can help provide these three foods for others, but only after we are able to receive them for ourselves. Then we can share the food with others. We can provide good food, good impressions and a finer quality of air. When we breathe consciously we are receiving the food we need and helping provide this food to others. First we need to do it, then we can help others. First we need to have being, then we can share it with others.

We have to gain something ourselves, which we do not as yet have, and that is a permanent being, a 'permanent I', or soul. It usually bothers people to hear this, but one is not born with a soul. We have a soul in potential, but it is not necessarily born yet. The birth of Christ is the symbol of this birth. We have an animal soul already, and we have a vegetable soul, but not necessarily a real human soul. What this means is that we have to gain it, as with Plato's 'immortal soul', or give birth to it, as in the birth of Christ. The substance of the soul comes into being through sacrifice. If we really want to know what this is and who we are, then we must continuously surrender, turning inside ourselves to our Lord, whatever that means to us individually. It is a continuous turning in the question of who we really are.

The esoteric aspect of this Work is to be able to die consciously each and every moment, and this serves the world in a particular way. As we die to our illusions a little more each day, a certain kind of energy is made available for the conscious evolution of mankind. Can you accept the fact that you don't know who you are? Nobody does totally, because only God knows the ultimate truth. It is for God to know and for us to question. So we need to question, 'Who am I?' Through this ultimate question, and the yearning to know the answer, the substance of the soul begins to come into being. Something comes about through the sacrifice of our self-concepts and our concepts of all things of this world, which are the illusions of the world, the shadow world of the real world. What starts to come about is the substance of the soul coming into being.

The only way to discover your real self is to give up the old self, surrendering all that you think you are. A 'permanent I', or soul, is gained when we sacrifice these illusions of who we are. This is the meaning of conscious death and why sacrifice is important. The substance of sacrifice becomes the substance of the permanent body, and every time we make a conscious sacrifice in love, this substance is released for the whole planet to use. This is part of an inner law concerning the reciprocal maintenance of the planet. If we come together in a group we can sacrifice ourselves to the centre. If we come to a teacher in humility, with both hands open and free, we are making a sacrifice. If we can love and serve another without trying to get something for ourselves, we are creating that substance of sacrifice.

This invisible substance of the permanent body is made from sacrifice and conscious death. This substance comes about through love, because every time we love properly there is sacrifice. If we are not prepared to die, then there is no real love. To love means to be awake, to be awake wherever we are and whatever we are doing. The 'permanent I', or the soul, is unborn until it is realized, and this is dependent upon our degree of awareness. The soul is a knowing substance, and in this knowing we come into love. It is the knowledge of who we are, and this inevitably leads to love.

What is left at the moment of conscious death is divisible into as many parts as are needed. The permanent body is not like our own sort of bubble which is fully enclosed and floats about separate from others. It is not like that; it interpenetrates. Every world above interpenetrates the worlds below. The great saints and masters of all time interpenetrate the space we are in. The physical body and concepts of the mind are what separate you from me, but the scent of the rose permeates a whole room. It is not a matter of you having your permanent body and I having mine. There is only One Being, and we can remain permanently conscious within that. The only way for this to come about is through sacrifice and conscious death, until ultimately there is no more you or me, but only the One. This is a great act of service, because what is left at that moment is divisible into as many parts as are needed. Then it is the everlasting bread of God, able to feed however many people are ready to receive it.

Death in Life

The understanding of death leads to eternal life.

To turn completely towards the truth is to surrender everything we think we are and everything we know. This is the great spiritual death, from which can emerge the real self. We need to make a great decision that we are prepared to die and from this death can come the freedom of being. Everything must go, all the resentment, envy and pride, all the fear, guilt and grief. Can we let it go? Do we want to let it go? Do we want to be free? Do we want to come into being? If we want to come into being, which means being completely free, we have to let go of everything, especially the past. We can't take it with us.

Our fear of letting go comes from our fear of death. The mind cannot face the fact of death, but if we can see that death is right around the corner, it will actually help us face life. We are all going to die at some point, so the facing of death could be one of the greatest things we ever do. The understanding of death leads to eternal life. Yet, this cannot be known intellectually. It has to be experienced, which means we have to die before we die. Then we will know that death is an illusion. We need to die to the concepts and illusions that are held so tightly out of fear, the fear of facing ourselves in the mirror of life.

Mevlana says, 'Come, come whoever you are'. The door is always open, but we can't take anything with us, because there has to be an empty space, a completely empty space in our hearts. Deep within us there is this longing to return to the One Source, to die to everything, all the anger, all the suffering and everything that holds us back from our freedom to be who we really are. We can return and come into the knowledge of love, but first we have to let go of all that stands in the way. We have to want this so much that we are willing to give our lives to it. The arms of God await us, but we have to make the first step. We have to want the truth with all our hearts or we will not find it. The moment we honestly say 'I will', everything that stands in the way will begin to go, until only the truth remains. This is the key to unlocking the door of the heart.

The door of the heart can only be opened from the inside. No one can open it for us. The greatest teacher or healer in the world cannot open the door of our heart. He can knock on it, or show us the possibility of it being opened, but he cannot open it. When we are completely empty, it opens from within as an act of grace. We can only knock on the door of the heart ourselves and ask that it be opened. We cannot open it, but we can help God open it from the inside. We do this by surrendering ourselves to God, to love. We can prepare for it through study and through yearning, but the actual opening is by grace and through our surrender in it. The way of love is always open. In reality the door is always open, but we cannot enter with all our preconceptions and opinions about what is inside.

We cannot know what is inside until we leave everything else outside. We have to leave everything behind. We can't take it with us. We can only enter in complete emptiness and abandonment. We want to approach God with absolute purity, so that nothing can stand in the way. We do this in love and for love, and little by little love melts the mind and the heart, until there is nothing but love. There is nothing else to hold on to. This is real freedom. The veils are lifted and we can truly say, 'Oh Thou!'

The doors open for us when we are completely empty, and in this emptiness we are free. We come into the freedom that already exists. All we can do is surrender more and more of ourselves to the freedom that already exists. When we can surrender all that we think we are, we become awake to the stream of life that pervades through all things. In freedom we can be awake to the all-pervading life flowing freely through all time. Freedom is always here. It is the true heritage of the soul. It is what we really are, but nobody can bring us into freedom. No system can bring us into freedom, because all systems are based upon concepts of the truth, which can bring us to the edge of realization, but cannot make it happen. We have to jump off on our own. We have to leave everything behind and jump off into freedom. Most people will hang onto the edge, but only those who surrender everything can find the freedom that awaits them. This is the knowledge of eternity and is the realization of freedom.

This freedom is beyond anybody's concept of what it might be. You come into Being. You come into the One Being which longs to come into being. There is only One Absolute Being. There is only One Teacher. It manifests through different people in different ways, but still, there is only One. As St. Francis said, 'What you are looking for is what is looking.' And when you come into Being, you will manifest exactly what is needed to manifest because there is nothing between you and your Lord. Inayat Khan said, 'Make God a reality and He will make you the truth.' Then, Being is free to come into being.

Freedom is totally surrendering to allow the free flow of life itself. It is not getting free of being in the body or being in the world. It is not freedom from, but freedom within, life. Freedom is allowing the free flow of love to manifest in our lives and in all the kingdoms on earth. We cannot taste this freedom if we are enslaved by the tyranny of thoughts and emotions that make us forget our true identity. The body, the feelings and the mind are gifts of God given to us to realize and manifest love on earth. If they tyrannize us we are not yet free to allow love to flow in the way it is intended.

We have to break through the systems and concepts, break through all the psychological types and belief systems. We have to break through astrology, go beyond our chart and our planets and everything that defines us. These systems are useful to some extent, and they can lead us to a degree of knowledge, but ultimately they will hold us back from real knowledge of ourselves, which can only come about through the surrender of all that we think we are.

Most people are afraid to take this plunge into the unknown. They want the security of thinking that they already know themselves and what life is about, because the unknown is too frightening and it takes too much work to question and observe oneself. They want others to tell them who they are. They want to find themselves in some book, because they are afraid to face themselves in the mirror and see the reality face to face. I would not tell you who you are even if you wanted me to. That would be a great disservice. But I will leave you with the question of who you are and if you have the courage to ask it yourself, the answer may unfold itself every moment of your life.

This Way is not easy. It can be very tough. And we have to be willing to give up something, which is ourselves. We have to be willing to go through a death of ourselves, in order to come into union with God. It is possible to come into union before we die, which is knowledge of the unity of God. We can have a taste of this conscious death in life, so that we can come to understand the nature of life itself. This requires great effort and we can't just leave it to God. That is not the answer to our lives at all. We have to work on ourselves. We have to do something ourselves. We have to make the first step, and we have to continue making that first step, because there is only one moment. In that step, we die. Yet God gave us free will, so we don't have to take that step. There is no compulsion here. It is up to us.

There is a story told by the great Sufi Farid ud-Din Attar. The phoenix is a lovely bird which lives in Hindustan. It has no mate and lives alone. Its beak, which is very hard and long, is pierced like a flute with nearly a hundred holes. Each of these holes gives out a sound, and in each sound is a particular secret. Sometimes he makes music through the holes, and when the birds and the fishes hear his sweet notes they become agitated, while the most ferocious beasts are in rapture. Then they all become silent. A philosopher once visited this bird and learned from him the science of music. The phoenix lives approximately a thousand years and he knows exactly the days of his death. So when his time comes he gathers around him a number of palm leaves and, distraught among the leaves, utters plaintive cries. From the openings of his beak he sends forth varied notes, and this music is drawn from the depths of his heart. His lamentations express the pain of his death and he trembles like a leaf. At the sound of his trumpet the birds and the beasts draw near to assist at the spectacle, and soon many fall into bewilderment. While the phoenix still has breath he beats his wings and ruffles his feathers so much that he produces a fire. The fire spreads and engulfs the phoenix, and soon it is reduced to living coals and then to ashes. Then, when the last spark has flickered out a new phoenix rises from the ashes.

There is a purpose to life, an honest to God purpose, and that is to die. Everybody is going to die at some point in their life, but how many of us have the courage to die? I offer this to you as a challenge. Do you have the courage to die? To die completely to the mind, to the ego, to the concepts? To die, not to escape life, but in order to really live and be more of service to God and mankind? Can we accept the challenge to die to every single concept we have ever known—all systems, all gurus, all teachers and everything, in order to come upon the truth itself which made it all possible? This is the challenge of our time.

We are all on the verge of death. At any one moment we are all facing the possibility of death. That is difficult to face but it's true. If we can be awake to the moment of death and go through it consciously, then we can help others through this last barrier. I am not talking about suicide or something morbid. I know death is the hardest thing to face. But if we can face it and go through it, which means surrendering everything of ourselves up to God, then we will find freedom.

What is ignorance? It is merely a lack of the knowledge of who we are. Do we want to die like that? Do we want to die ignorant? I don't. I hope you don't. But as we walk out of the door, we may die. Do we wish to come into realization before we die?

Death is lingering around the corner. Death is right behind us, waiting. I'm not joking. Sooner or later, we are going to be confronted with death. And then what? What will we do when we face death? Who will we turn to? Will we turn to our special guide or to our special practice? Is channeling going to help us? Are golden rays or pink rays or mantras going to change anything? At that point of death we can only really turn to the truth. When we are on our death bed, we are going to have to face the truth. We will want to know who we are and who is our Lord. We will want to dissolve in love with our Lord. We will want union.

We might aspire to be like Mevlana, who ceased to exist outside of God. This does not mean being outside of life. It means being totally committed in life and to life, and Mevlana described it thus: 'Until thou becometh thou will not know it completely, whether it be light or darkness. If thou become reason thou will know reason perfectly. If thou become love thou will know love's flaming wick.' Our aspiration is not for ourselves, but for God, in the knowledge of the unity of God. We might even ask, 'May I be allowed to die now?' Upon hearing this a close brother of mine said to me, 'I don't know if I'm ready for that', and I replied, 'Does anybody know whether or not they're ready for it?' We certainly need courage.

Through death come resurrection. Our goal is resurrection, and death leads us to resurrection. But before we can come into resurrection, there needs to be recognition, which is the recognition of One Absolute Being behind all beings. With recognition it is possible to die before you die. This leads to redemption, and then to resurrection. What other way can you die except through recognition? Consider love. Consider lovers. How can you die in love without first recognizing it, without first knowing you are loved? How can you be redeemed in love without dying in love? You all really want to die in love. You all want to know you are loved. God is the lover and you are the beloved. Then you become the lover and God is the Beloved. And finally there is no separation, so that God is both the lover and the Beloved. In God we die in love and in God we are born in love. When you die in love there is only love remaining. The lover and the beloved cease to exist apart from each other, for there is only love.

Reason is powerless in the expression of love. Love alone
is capable of revealing the truth of love and of being a lover.
The way of our prophets is a way of truth. If you want
to live, die in love. Die in love, if you want to remain alive.
MEVLANA JALALUDDIN RUMI